STECK-VAUGHN EN PAREJAS™

FICTION AND NONFICTION FOR EMERGENT READERS

TEACHER'S GUIDE

Stage 2

Bilingual/ESL version of Teacher's Guide
Rubí Borgia

Consultant

Eleanor W. Thonis
Bilingual Consultant
State Department of Education
Sacramento, CA

Reviewers

Concepción D. Guerra
Bilingual/ESL Education Director
Pharr-San Juan-Alamo Independent School District
Pharr, TX

Lucrecia G. Gutiérrez
Literacy Specialist & Bilingual Consultant
Newark Public Schools
Newark, NJ

María Núñez-Hernando
Bilingual/ESOL Teacher
Ridgewood Park Elementary School
Orlando, FL

STECK-VAUGHN COMPANY®
A Division of Harcourt Brace & Company

ACKNOWLEDGMENTS

Executive Editor	Stephanie Muller
Senior Editor	Amanda Sperry
Editors	Kathleen Gower
	Gabriela Prati
Supervising Designer	Pamela Heaney
Electronic Production Artists	Donna Brawley
	Isabel Garza
Electronic Production Specialist	Alan Klemp

Photography: (abbreviations: AA: Animals Animals; FPG: FPG International; GH: Grant Heilman Photography; PA: Peter Arnold, Inc.; PE: PhotoEdit; SB: Stock Boston; TSM: The Stock Market; TSI: Tony Stone Images)

Front Cover: (tl) Courtesy NASA, (tr) ©Uniphoto, (m) ©Mickey Gibson/AA, (bl) ©Jeff Rotman/PA, (br) ©Andy Rouse/DRK Photo; Back Cover: (tl) ©Gerard Lacz/PA, (tr) ©Ted Levin/AA, (ml) ©Glen Allison/TSI, (m) ©Daniel Cox/TSI, (mr) ©Zefa Germany/TSM; p.1 (tl) ©Mickey Gibson/AA; p.1 (bl) ©Glen Allison/TSI; p.2 (tl) ©Zefa Germany/TSM; p.2 (tr) ©John Lei/SB; p.2 (b) ©G. Kinns/Natural Science Photos; p.3 (tr) ©Glen Allison/TSI; p.3 (m) ©Uniphoto; p.3 (bl) ©Andy Rouse/DRK Photo; p.3 (br) ©Daniel Cox/TSI; p.4 (l) ©Josef Beck/FPG; p. 4 (tr) Park Street; p.4 (br) ©Jeff Rotman/PA; p.5 (t) Park Street; p.5 (bl) ©Ted Levin/AA; p.5 (br) ©Uniphoto; p.6 ©Glen Allison/TSI; p.8 (l) Park Street; p.8 (r) ©Gerard Lacz/PA; p.9 (t) Park Street; p.9 (m) ©Josef Beck/FPG; p.9 (b) ©John Lei/SB; p.10 Park Street; p.11 (t) ©Bob Daemrich/SB; p.11 (m) ©Diane Lowe/SB; p.11 (b) Park Street; p.12 (t) ©Josef Beck/FPG; p.12 (b) Park Street; p.13 (t, inset) ©Glen Allison/TSI; p.13 (t, background) ©Grant Heilman/GH; p.13 (b) ©Larry Lefever/GH; p.15 (t) ©Glen Allison/TSI; p.15 (b) ©Barry Runk/GH; p.16 (t, inset) ©Glen Allison/TSI; p.16 (t, background) ©Grant Heilman/GH; p.19 (t) ©Manfred Mehlig/TSI; p. 19 (b) ©Daniel Cox/TSI; p.21 (t) ©Tom Ulrich/TSI; p. 21 (b) ©Steve Kaufman/PA; p. 22 (t) ©Manfred Mehlig/TSI; p. 25 (t) ©Larry Lefever/GH; p. 25 (b) ©Runk, Schoenberger/GH; p. 27 (t) ©Ted Levin/AA; p. 27 (b) ©Grant Heilman/GH; p.28 (t) ©Larry Lefever/GH; p.30 ©Grant Heilman/GH; p.31 (both) ©Chuck Davis/TSI; p.33 (t) ©Stuart Westmorland/TSI; p.33 (b) ©Jeff Rotman/PA; p. 34 (t) ©Chuck Davis/TSI; p.37 (t) ©NASA/SB; p.37 (b) ©E.R. Degginger/Earth Scenes; p.39 (t) ©James L. Amos/PA; p.39 (b) Courtesy NASA; p.40 (t) ©NASA/SB; p.43 (t) ©Image Bank; p.43 (b) ©Joseph Devenney/Image Bank; p.45 (t) ©Kevin Schafer/PA; p.45 (b) ©Mickey Gibson/AA; p.46 (t) ©Image Bank; pp.49 (both), 51 (t) Courtesy NASA; p.51 (b) ©Richard Pasley/SB; p.52 (t) Courtesy NASA; p.55 (t) ©Josef Beck/FPG; p.55 (b) ©John Lei/SB; p.57 (t) ©Bob Daemrich/SB; p.57 (b) ©Diane Lowe/SB; p.58 (t) ©Josef Beck/FPG; p.61 (t) ©Ken Reid/FPG; p.61 (b) ©Cathlyn Melloan/TSI; p.63 (t) ©Roland Seitre/PA; p.63 (b) ©American Museum of Natural History; p.64 (t) ©Ken Reid/FPG; p.67 (t) ©Johnny Johnson/DRK Photo; p.67 (b) ©Frank Siteman/SB; p.69 (t) ©Alan G. Nelson/AA; p.69 (b) ©Lynn M. Stone/DRK Photo; p.70 (t) ©Johnny Johnson/DRK Photo.

Illustrations: Cindy Aarvig, Layne Lundstrom, David Chapman

En parejas™ is a trademark of Steck-Vaughn Company.

ISBN: 0-7398-0742-0

©2000 Steck-Vaughn Company

Steck-Vaughn Company grants you permission to duplicate enough copies of blackline masters to distribute to your students. All other material contained in this publication may not be reproduced or utilized in any form or by any means, electronic or mechanical, including photocopying, recording, or by any information storage and retrieval system, without permission in writing from the copyright owner. Requests for permission to make copies of any part of the work should be mailed to: Copyright Permissions, Steck-Vaughn Company, P.O. Box 26015, Austin, Texas 78755.

Printed in the United States of America.

1 2 3 4 5 6 7 8 9 10 SEG 03 02 01 00 99

CONTENTS

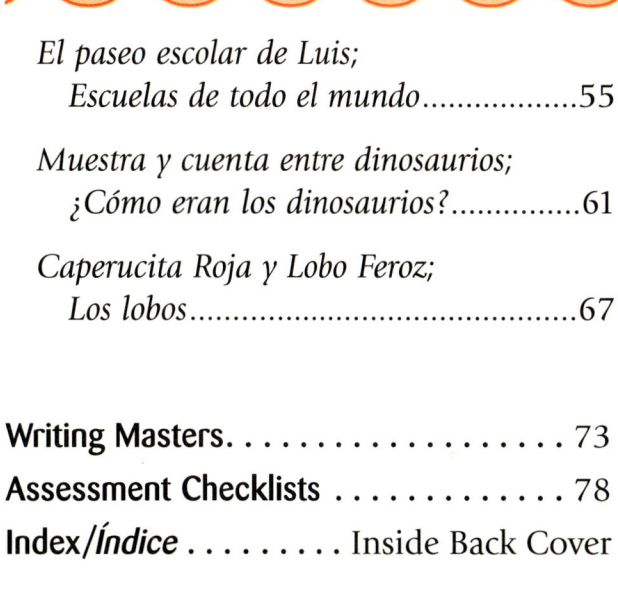

Program Overview 4
Types of Reading. 5
Program Components 6
Topics and Skills Chart 7
Assessment. 8
A Sample Lesson. 9

Lessons, Tie It to English, and *Llévame a casa* Activity Pages

Pasteles de manzana en familia;
  Manzanas y más manzanas 13

El regreso de Ricitos de Oro;
  ¿Quién vive en el bosque? 19

Las estaciones de Esteban;
  Las estaciones del año 25

El pez maravilloso;
  Los grandes tiburones blancos 31

La luna adormecedora;
  El hombre en la Luna 37

El concurso de castillos de arena;
  Criaturas de la playa 43

Podré ser lo que quiera;
  ¡Despegue! 49

El paseo escolar de Luis;
  Escuelas de todo el mundo 55

Muestra y cuenta entre dinosaurios;
  ¿Cómo eran los dinosaurios? 61

Caperucita Roja y Lobo Feroz;
  Los lobos 67

Writing Masters. 73
Assessment Checklists 78
Index/*Índice* . . . . Inside Back Cover

PROGRAM OVERVIEW

Children love hearing and sharing stories. There are many wonderful stories to share with your children. But did you ever notice that after you share a great story about fish, children want to know more about real fish? Suddenly you find yourself needing an informative book about fish. A simple nonfiction book that is on the same level and is as interesting as the story book would be very useful. This pairing is part of the Steck-Vaughn *EN PAREJAS*™ series. *EN PAREJAS* is an emergent reading program with fiction and nonfiction books paired together by matching themes and topics.

EN PAREJAS opens the exciting world of reading for both pleasure and information. This series of books helps children make the transition from reading narrative texts to reading informational texts. You can keep the interest in a topic alive as you help children learn to read a nonfiction companion book. With *EN PAREJAS* children can explore nonfiction themes or topics through factual books that they can read. In addition, learning to read nonfiction prepares children for some standardized tests.

Using paired books makes teaching reading skills easier. Since children use some of the same strategies to read both kinds of texts, you can continue to teach and reinforce reading skills while children explore new texts. Each pair of books contains patterned language and strong matching of print and illustrations or photos to support emergent readers. The common content of both books, with their base in familiar topics, allows readers to use prior knowledge and build on what they know. Reading informational texts becomes an extension of reading fictional narratives, no longer appearing as a new or difficult reading experience. The books also work as models for writing. Children can easily model their own writings on these predictable and comfortable books.

The *Lectores principiantes, segunda etapa* books, each with sixteen pages, are slightly more difficult and have more complex information than those found in *Lectores principiantes, primera etapa* which consist of eight-page books. Children build on the reading strategies they developed in *Lectores principiantes, primera etapa*. Thus, *EN PAREJAS* builds confident readers and writers of both narrative and informational texts. For teachers, the convenience of having books already paired will save valuable planning time.

CLASSROOM MANAGEMENT

There are three ways to use *EN PAREJAS* books in the classroom.

1. Whole Class Instruction. You may demonstrate specific reading strategies or share books with the whole class.
2. Group Instruction. Specific program components may be used to teach a reading strategy, language pattern, or phonics focus to groups of children.
3. Paired or Independent Instruction. Children work in pairs or independently using selected books from the program.

TYPES OF READING

SHARED READING

Shared reading helps children hear language and how it works in different kinds of texts. When a Big Book or one of the small books is read aloud, children can focus on listening to the author's words. They listen for language patterns, story structure, and the sounds of words. They look at illustrations and photos to enrich their reading experience. As the text becomes more familiar, children can begin to participate in the reading by joining in or echoing words from the text. After the book has been shared over and over, children feeling comfortable with the story may be able to read the text independently.

GUIDED READING

Guided reading helps children use strategies to become independent readers. It allows children to encounter reading strategies that enable them to read for enjoyment and meaning, understand basic conventions of print, and become familiar with cues to access more complex text.

Guided reading begins with an introduction to the book. This may be done by using a question-and-answer format to access children's prior knowledge. A picture walk usually follows, taking children through the story or information in the book. Children discuss what they see in the pictures and discuss their knowledge about the topic. Involve children in making predictions about what will happen next and in predicting a word in a sentence. This gives children insight in developing independent strategies of making and confirming predictions. Children should also be given any support that will allow them to handle tricky parts of the text.

The next step is reading the book. Children will read the book as independently as possible. This may sound like choral reading, but children are working independently. During this reading, make sure children are on task, supporting individuals when necessary. If children have developed the skill to read aloud well, try having them read silently.

The guided reading lesson may include a follow-up activity. Follow-up activities can be art, writing, or discussions that pertain to the text of the book. Guided reading helps children take ownership of strategies that they can apply to other books so that reading becomes independent.

DIRECTED READING

Directed reading helps children build skills and strategies. Mini lessons, presenting a specific reading strategy, can be used with a small group of children or a large group. The mini lessons are used to build skills in the areas of reading comprehension, language patterns, and phonics. In the rereading of a text, children focus on a particular skill or feature. Once children are familiar with the text, directed reading can be done at any time.

INDEPENDENT READING

Independent reading can occur when children are able to read particular books on their own and want to select and read them unassisted. Independent reading also allows children to practice the reading strategies they have developed. Rereading familiar books gives children confidence and promotes self-esteem.

PROGRAM COMPONENTS

EN PAREJAS STUDENT BOOKS

There are twenty reading books, or ten topic-based pairs, in *Lectores principiantes, segunda etapa*. In each pair, one title is fiction and one is nonfiction. Several pairs may be combined to present a particular theme to children. For example, an animals thematic unit could include the pairs on fish, beach creatures, wolves, and even dinosaurs.

These emergent-level books provide opportunities for children to read independently, in cooperative groups, and as a whole class. The books are written so that they can be used as models for the children to write their own stories and facts.

BIG BOOKS

The four Big Books in this program can be used for shared reading in small- and large-group lessons and demonstrations. Children will love to join in and read along with these stories and will be fascinated by the illustrations, photos, and information. The Big Books can also be used to point out examples from the skills lessons, provide motivation for follow-up activities, and serve as models for writing. They also help children recognize story structures, understand literary concepts, and develop questions in response to reading.

TEACHER'S GUIDE

An 80-page teacher's guide has lessons that develop skills for each pair of books, such as phonics, reading strategies, and language patterns. The teacher's guide also provides home activities, assessment checklists, and blackline masters for each book pair. The guide has a flexible format that allows teachers to select books and lessons as needed, in the order that suits classroom needs and current themes. The order of lessons in this guide is based on the increasing level of difficulty of each book pair.

AUDIO TAPES

Each book is accompanied by an audio cassette tape. The audio tapes are ideal for reading centers where children can listen to a tape and read along in their books. A brief introduction keys the listener into the topic of the book, and the closing asks a question for the reader to think about after hearing the text.

TIE IT TO ENGLISH

For each pair of books, there is an English language development blackline master that ties in elements of the theme to basic English vocabulary or language functions. These fun activities motivate children to transfer their Spanish listening, speaking, reading, writing, and viewing skills to English.

LLÉVAME A CASA ACTIVITIES

Each book pair has a family activity master in Spanish. These masters contain easy-to-do activities for family members and the child. Each activity is intended to extend and enrich the child's print awareness and beginning reading experiences.

TOPICS AND SKILLS CHART

EN PAREJAS Titles	*EN PAREJAS* Topics	Reading Strategies	Language Patterns	Phonics Focus
Pasteles de manzana en familia and *Manzanas y más manzanas*	Apples *Las manzanas*	• Retelling events in sequence • Using context to identify key words	• Using action words • Modifying plurals to singular forms	• Identifying the initial and medial /l/ sound • Identifying *r* consonant blends
El regreso de Ricitos de Oro and *¿Quién vive en el bosque?*	Woods or Forests *Los bosques*	• Identifying comparisons and contrasts • Recognizing setting	• Locating dialogue verbs • Identifying naming words	• Reviewing the initial /r/ sound • Identifying *que, qui* and *gue, gui* combinations
Las estaciones de Esteban and *Las estaciones del año*	Seasons of the Year *Las estaciones del año*	• Demonstrating story sequence • Identifying cause and effect	• Applying action words • Recognizing names of the seasons	• Identifying final vowels with accents • Identifying the /ñ/ sound
El pez maravilloso and *Los grandes tiburones blancos*	Fish *Los peces*	• Recalling sequence • Classifying information	• Identifying repetitive dialogue • Using question-and-answer format	• Identifying the /s/ sound in the initial, medial, and final positions • Identifying the /k/ sound before the vowels *a*, *o*, and *u*
La luna adormecedora and *El hombre en la Luna*	Moon *La Luna*	• Making inferences about characters • Distinguishing between fact and fiction	• Recognizing rhyming words • Using question-and-answer format	• Understanding rhyme • Identifying questioning intonation
El concurso de castillos de arena and *Criaturas de la playa*	Beaches *La playa*	• Demonstrating how pictures tell a story • Defining key words using context clues	• Using describing words • Separating compound words	• Identifying words with four syllables • Identifying the /pl/ sound
Podré ser lo que quiera and *¡Despegue!*	Careers *Las profesiones*	• Making inferences • Making generalizations	• Identifying naming words • Identifying describing words	• Identifying the medial /r/ sound between vowels • Reviewing *r* blends
El paseo escolar de Luis and *Escuelas de todo el mundo*	Schools *Las escuelas*	• Summarizing the story • Comparing and contrasting experiences	• Identifying naming words • Identifying action words	• Identifying the digraphs *ch* and *ll* • Identifying diphthongs
Muestra y cuenta entre dinosaurios and *¿Cómo eran los dinosaurios?*	Dinosaurs *Los dinosaurios*	• Identifying categories • Recognizing comparisons	• Identifying repetitive dialogue • Identifying naming words	• Reviewing the /y/ sound • Reviewing the /l/ sound in the initial and medial positions
Caperucita Roja y Lobo Feroz and *Los lobos*	Wolves *Los lobos*	• Predicting outcomes • Categorizing information	• Demonstrating use of dialogue • Identifying plural words	• Reviewing the /r/ sound • Reviewing the /b/ sound

ASSESSMENT

Many methods of assessment can be used with *EN PAREJAS*. The most valuable assessment tool may be listening to children read and observing how they use the books. Ideas for observations and suggestions for portfolio items are included in the activities and skills lessons for each pair of books.

Allow children to self-select titles, noticing how they approach the books. Ask them to point out the book cover, title, and author's name. Note whether they start with a fiction or a nonfiction title and whether they can tell how the books are different. In order to observe these things, make sure the books are accessible to the children. Keep them in a location where children can easily find them and make selections. Next to the books, you may want to keep a list of the titles so children can write comments, their initials, or a symbol, such as a happy face, if they would recommend the title.

During lesson introductions and Before Reading activities, children are asked to name what they know about a topic and to predict what they might read about in the book. Always list, date, and initial children's responses. This will allow them to ask questions of each other when working in groups and to verify or change any predictions they may have made about the topic or books. This work should be saved and referred to throughout the lesson. These lists and comments can also be used to complete a chart: What We Know *(Lo que sabemos)*, What We Want to Know *(Lo que queremos saber)*, and What We Learned *(Lo que aprendimos)*.

Use the *EN PAREJAS Assessment Checklists* to observe children's progress. These evaluations can be included in children's portfolios. The checklists can also be used during conferences with each child. Use the lists as starting points to talk about reading and writing and how children feel they are doing.

The *EN PAREJAS* books provide many models for children's own writing. Look to see if the various patterns in texts are replicated in children's writing. Encourage children to work in pairs or independently to develop stories. Set aside time for children to read their writing aloud so you can hear how they are using language.

The work children do on lesson activities and projects can also be included in their portfolios. As children do projects, it may be helpful to have a project display table. Children can display their projects as they work on them. This allows them to explain to the other children what they are doing. As they explain their projects, listen to see if they understand the tasks, activities, and targeted skills.

8

A SAMPLE LESSON

INTRODUCING *EN PAREJAS*
The four-page lesson for each pair of books is the instructional core of the *EN PAREJAS* program.

The teacher introduces the topic or theme of a book pair. Children tell what they know about the topic (activating prior knowledge), talk about their relevant personal experiences, and connect their reading of the new books to prior reading. Four Big Books are available for introducing selected books.

A synopsis for each book provides a quick reference when selecting titles or introducing books to children.

Every book has three stated instructional objectives. For each *Reading Strategy*, *Language Pattern*, and *Phonics Focus*, a mini lesson targets a specific skill area.

The Spanish language key words from each book tie directly to lesson objectives. These words can be used for vocabulary development or as key story words. Children may also use these words to make a story dictionary after they have read the books.

INTRODUCING *EN PAREJAS*
Invite children to describe what they know about their school. (*Descríbanme qué saben de su escuela.*) List their ideas on the board or on chart paper. Ask them to name types of things they enjoy at school. (*Díganme cuáles son las actividades que disfrutan en la escuela.*) Display the two books, and encourage children to tell what they know about them from the titles and pictures on the book covers. (*¿Qué pueden decir de estos libros al mirar las ilustraciones y las portadas?*)

El paseo escolar de Luis
On the day of the class field trip to the zoo, Luis has difficulty keeping track of his lunch box. In the end, Luis enjoys lunch at the zoo after all.

Key Words:
el mono
el elefante
la cebra
la jirafa

Objectives:
Reading Strategy: Summarizing the story
Language Pattern: Identifying naming words
Phonics Focus: Identifying the digraphs *ch* and *ll*

Escuelas de todo el mundo
This photo essay provides children opportunities to compare and contrast their own school experiences with those of school children around the world.

Key Words:
caminamos
visitamos
usamos
escribimos
aprendemos
practicamos

Objectives:
Reading Strategy: Comparing and contrasting experiences
Language Pattern: Identifying action words
Phonics Focus: Identifying diphthongs

Additional Components:
Audio Cassette Tape: *El paseo escolar de Luis*
Escuelas de todo el mundo
Writing Masters, pages 73–77

Other Books About Schools
Me gustan los libros, Liliana Santirso
Timoteo va a la escuela, Rosemary Wells

55

The *Additional Components* list tells at a glance what accompanying materials can be used with this lesson.

Ten audio cassette tapes are available for use with all twenty of the *EN PAREJAS* books in *Lectores principiantes, segunda etapa*.

Each lesson includes a list of additional books in Spanish on the topic. All of these books are readily available in the United States.

Big Books are available for four of the books in the program. Big Books are especially helpful for whole lessons when the teacher is demonstrating a reading strategy, illustrating a text pattern, or sharing language.

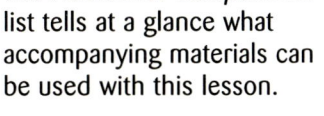

READING THE BOOKS

Before children begin to read, the teacher discusses the book cover and points out the title, author, and illustrator. Children are asked to predict what they think will happen in the book. The teacher can list, date, and initial responses and save them for use later in the lesson.

The teacher uses children's predictions about what will happen in the book to set a purpose for reading. The teacher then asks a set of questions to guide the reading and to help children frame their thinking as they read.

After reading the book, children follow up on their pre-reading predictions and talk about what they learned. Here they tell how the book is like or unlike other books they have read on the topic. They are also given opportunities to discuss opinions about the book contents, characters, art, and photos.

There are response activities for each book. One may be a reading response activity, for children to personally react to the book. Another may be a writing activity for extending the book or applying the text patterns.

El paseo escolar de Luis

BEFORE READING

Ask children to tell about a school trip they have taken. What was it like? Did they lose anything? *(Cuéntenme sobre algún paseo escolar al que hayan ido. ¿Cómo fue el paseo? ¿Se les perdió algo?)* Show the cover of the book, read the title, and ask children to predict what they think will happen. *(Miren la cubierta del libro, lean el título y díganme sobre qué creen que tratará el libro.)*

READING

Set a purpose for reading by asking children to think about where Luis' class might be going. *(¿Adónde creen que va la clase de Luis?)* Encourage them to connect happenings in the book to occurrences in their everyday lives.

Use questions such as these to guide the reading: 
- ¿Cómo se siente uno cuando está tan alegre que no puede pensar?
- ¿Qué creen que piensan el papá, la maestra y el chofer del autobús cuando le entregan la lonchera a Luis?
- ¿Por qué pensó Luis que el elefante, la cebra y la jirafa se estaban comiendo su almuerzo?

AFTER READING

Ask children how they think Luis felt when he found his lunch and backpack. *(¿Cómo creen que se sintió Luis cuando encontró su mochila y su almuerzo?)* Invite children to brainstorm other ways Luis could have kept track of his lunch box. *(Quiero que piensen en algunas formas en que Luis hubiera podido seguirle el rastro a su lonchera.)*

Response Activities

Too Happy to Think!
Materials: drawing paper, markers

Remind children how the book began with the sentence, *¡Luis estaba tan alegre que no podía pensar!* Invite children to draw a picture of something they think Luis was happy about *(a particular animal, riding a bus, being with his friends, etc.)*. *(Dibujen algo por lo que Luis pudiera estar alegre [un animal en particular, pasear en autobús, estar con sus amigos, etc.].)* Then have children share their pictures. On the board make a list of their ideas about why Luis was so happy.

¡OJO! Although the word *lonchera* is borrowed from the English, it has become so popular and widely used that it is better known than the word *fiambrera*.

MINI LESSONS

• READING STRATEGY
Summarizing the Story

Ask children to tell about the story in one to three sentences: *La clase de Luis fue al zoológico. Luis perdió su almuerzo. Luis almorzó con todos.* Help children see how the sentences sum up the ideas of the story.

• LANGUAGE PATTERN
Identifying Naming Words

Have children recall words from the story that name animals: *los monos, los elefantes, las cebras, las jirafas.* Help children locate these words in the book. Ask them to describe strategies they used to locate each word. *(Díganme las estrategias que utilizaron para localizar cada palabra.)*

PHONICS FOCUS

Identifying the Digraphs ch and ll

Explain to children that double l (ll) and c, h (ch) are two letter combinations that represent a sound different from that of the original letters. *(La doble l (ll) y la c, h (ch) son dos combinaciones de letras que representan un sonido diferente al de las letras originales.)* Write examples on the board *(llorar, chaqueta).* Reread the story, asking children to clap once when they hear the ll combination and twice when they hear the ch combination. *(Den una palmada cada vez que oigan el sonido de la combinación de la doble l (ll) y dos palmadas cuando oigan el sonido de la combinación c y h (ch).)*

Many lessons offer a feature (¡OJO!) that informs teachers of lexical variations for many of the Spanish language vocabulary words used in the student books.

THE MINI LESSONS

Escuelas de todo el mundo

BEFORE READING

Invite children to tell what they know about schools in other countries. *(Cuenten lo que saben sobre las escuelas en otros países.)* Create a chart with the headings What We Know *(Lo que sabemos)* and What We Want to Know *(Lo que queremos saber)*. Then introduce the book. Ask children to look at the cover photograph to predict what they think they will learn about other schools. *(Miren la portada y díganme qué creen que aprenderán sobre otras escuelas.)*

READING

Tell children they will be reading a book in which the photographs provide much information about the setting and the life of school children all over the world. *(Van a leer un libro en el cual las fotografías les darán mucha información sobre el ambiente y la vida escolar de niños de todo el mundo.)* Guide them to compare these schools to their own experiences as they read.

Use questions such as these to guide the reading:
- ¿En qué se parecen tu escuela y las escuelas de los niños en el libro? ¿En qué son diferentes?
- ¿Cómo van ustedes a la escuela?
- ¿Cómo pasan el día en la escuela?

AFTER READING

Encourage children to tell what they learned about schools around the world. *(¿Qué han aprendido sobre las escuelas de todo el mundo?)* List their ideas on the chart paper from the Before Reading activity. Invite them to compare what they thought the book would be about to the list of what they learned. *(Comparen lo que ustedes pensaron que este libro iba a tratar con la lista de lo que aprendieron.)*

Response Activities

Where Is It?
Materials: world map

Locate the countries in *Escuelas de todo el mundo* on the world map. Invite groups of children to locate the country closest to the United States and also the country farthest away from the United States. *(Busquen el país que está más cerca de los Estados Unidos y también el país que está más lejos de los Estados Unidos.)*

MINI LESSONS

• READING STRATEGY
Comparing and Contrasting Experiences

Ask children what they learned from reading *Escuelas de todo el mundo*. *(¿Qué han aprendido de este libro?)* Have them tell how their own school experiences are similar or different. *(Díganme en qué las experiencias escolares son semejantes o diferentes a las de ustedes.)* Help children make some generalizations about how they are like children around the world.

• LANGUAGE PATTERN
Identifying Action Words

Write *caminamos* and *escribimos* on the board. Tell children that these words show a specific action. *(Estas palabras denotan una acción específica.)* Have children find other action words in the book. *(Busquen otras palabras de acción en el libro.)* Then ask volunteers to select one of these action words to pantomime as others try to guess the word.

PHONICS FOCUS

Identifying Diphthongs

Review with children that a diphthong is a combination of two vowels pronounced as one sound. *(Un diptongo es una combinación de dos vocales pronunciadas como un sólo sonido: ju__e__go, pat__io__.)* As you reread the story, ask children to say the word *¡diptongo!* every time they hear one. Write the following words on the board and call on volunteers to underline the letters forming each diphthong: esc__ue__la, n__ue__stra, __ai__re.

57

The mini lessons develop and reinforce the reading strategy, language pattern, and phonics objectives. These lessons can be used for direct reading instruction. The *Writing Masters* and *Assessment Checklists* provided at the end of the Teacher's Guide may be used with these mini lessons. These items can be added to children's portfolios.

The Reading Strategy mini lesson focuses on a reading comprehension skill, such as defining multiple meanings, sequencing, predicting outcomes, drawing conclusions, or making inferences.

The Language Pattern points out rhymes, repetitions, formats, and types of words used in context. These lessons help children recognize the different ways and patterns in which language is used.

The Phonics Focus identifies obvious phonic elements of the Spanish language text. This helps children learn phonics skills in context. These short activities are used to introduce children to phonic elements or to reinforce concepts already taught.

TYING THE PAIR TOGETHER

Finally, the two books in the topical pair are tied together. Children tell how the books are the same and how they are different. They can also tell what they have learned about the topic and share their work.

These activities are cross-curricular. Some include writing or song activities that encourage language development. Icons indicate whether an activity is recommended for an individual, a pair of children, or the whole class.

Tying the Pair Together

Display the two books and encourage children to compare and contrast them. Ask children how they are the same and different. *(Quiero que comparen estos dos libros. Díganme en qué son parecidos y en qué son diferentes.)* Have children share what they have learned about schools and field trips. *(Compartan lo que han aprendido sobre las escuelas y los paseos escolares.)*

Nutrition: What's for Lunch?
Materials: writing paper, pencils

Invite children to list foods they might take to school in a lunch box. *(Hagan una lista de los alimentos que ustedes llevarían a la escuela en una lonchera.)* Have them discuss the pictures in *El paseo escolar de Luis* and *Escuelas de todo el mundo* and talk about what other foods children might take to school. *(¿Qué alimentos creen que llevarían otros niños a la escuela?)* Lead them to understand that children around the world sometimes eat different kinds of food.

Science: What's the Weather?
Materials: copies of *El paseo escolar de Luis* and *Escuelas de todo el mundo*, paper

Encourage children to study the illustrations and photographs in both books to determine if the climate is hot or cold in each picture. *(Observen bien las ilustraciones y las fotografías en ambos libros para determinar si el clima es caliente o frío.)* Compare the climates in the different countries to the climate where Luis lives. *(Comparen el clima en los diferentes países con el clima donde vive Luis.)* Have children write a sentence about where they live and how it compares to one of the places in the photographs. *(Escriban una oración acerca del lugar donde viven y cómo se compara a una de estas fotografías.)*

Geography: Animals Around the World
Materials: books about animals, globe

Write the names of the countries from *Escuelas de todo el mundo* on the board. Together with children review the location of these countries on the world map or globe. Then ask children where they think the animals in *El paseo escolar de Luis* came from. *(¿De dónde creen que son los animales que aparecen en* El paseo escolar de Luis*?)* Use books about animals to discuss which animals might have come from which countries.

ASSESSMENT

- Ask children to tell what they have learned about different schools. Record and date these responses. *(¿Qué han aprendido sobre las diferentes escuelas?)*
- Review the objectives given in the lessons for *El paseo escolar de Luis* and *Escuelas de todo el mundo*. Place samples of children's work on the objectives in their portfolios.
- Use informal conferencing with children to assess reading, language, and phonics skills they have learned from the books.

Home Activities

Copy and distribute to children the *Llévame a casa* activity master found on page 60. Tell children to ask their families to describe the schools they attended in first grade. *(Pídanles a sus familias que describan las escuelas a las que ellos asistieron en primer grado.)*

58

The assessment suggestions provide ideas for children's portfolios and observations of progress. They can be used in conjunction with the checklists found on pages 78–80 in this guide. Also see page 8 for ways to use *En Parejas* for assessment.

Each lesson is followed by reproducible blackline masters for Tie It to English activities, and a *Llévame a casa* activity letter provided in Spanish.

12

INTRODUCING *EN PAREJAS*

To introduce the books in this pair, display the book covers. Have children tell which cover shows a drawing and which shows a photograph. *(Díganme cuál cubierta tiene un dibujo y cuál cubierta tiene una fotografía.)* Ask children which apples they think look tastiest, and discuss why. *(¿Cuál de las manzanas se ve más sabrosa? ¿Por qué?)* Draw an apple on the board and invite children to create a word web around the word *manzana*, using descriptive words such as *dulce, roja, jugosa,* and *crujiente*.

Pasteles de manzana en familia

On a visit to Abuelito and Abuelita's farm, a family picks, washes, and peels apples with the aid of special machines. The grandparents' amazing machines then turn the apples into pies for everyone to enjoy.

Key Words:
recogerlas   lavamos
pelamos   cernimos
echamos   amasamos

Objectives:
Reading Strategy: Retelling events in sequence
Language Pattern: Using action words
Phonics Focus: Identifying the initial and medial /l/ sound

Manzanas y más manzanas

A photo essay tells how apples are raised from seeds to harvest. After the apples go to market, they are turned into a variety of products.

Key Words:
las manzanas   los huertos
las semillas   los manzanos
las flores   los postres

Objectives:
Reading Strategy: Using context to identify key words
Language Pattern: Modifying plurals to singular forms
Phonics Focus: Identifying *r* consonant blends

Additional Components:

Audio Cassette Tape: *Pasteles de manzana en familia*
Manzanas y más manzanas
Writing Masters, pages 73–77

Other Books About Apples

La canción del manzano, Jaroslav Seifert
El poni, el oso y el manzano, Sigrid Heuck

13

Pasteles de manzana
en familia

BEFORE READING

Ask children, *¿Cuáles son algunos de los postres de manzanas que más les gustan?* List children's responses on a chart, and invite them to add illustrations. Display the cover of the book and read aloud the title. Ask children, *¿Qué creen que ocurrirá en este cuento?*

READING

Help children set a purpose for reading. Have them tell how knowing the order of events helps them understand what they are reading. As they read, encourage children to think about the steps involved in preparing apples to make apple pie. *(Piensen sobre los pasos que deben seguirse para preparar las manzanas para hacer un pastel de manzana.)*

Use questions such as these to guide the reading:
- *¿Por qué abuelito y abuelita cultivan manzanas?*
- *¿Quién está trabajando más para preparar las manzanas?*
- *¿Quién hizo estas máquinas?*
- *¿Les gustan las manzanas a todos los personajes del libro? ¿Cómo lo saben?*

AFTER READING

Discuss *Pasteles de manzana en familia*. Ask children what they now know about making apple pies. *(¿Qué saben ahora que no sabían antes sobre los pasteles de manzana?)* Review the children's Before Reading predictions.

Response Activities

Another Invention
Materials: large sheets of paper for a mural, crayons

Ask children to think of a machine they could invent for cleaning up after all the pie has been eaten. *(Piensen en una máquina que podrían inventar para limpiar después que se han comido todos los pasteles.)* Lead them in a discussion to brainstorm different features of the machine and to give it a name. Then have children work together to draw the machine on a mural.

Write a Recipe
Materials: paper, pencils, copies of *Pasteles de manzana en familia*

Using the story as a reference, have children work in pairs to write instructions for an apple pie recipe. Have them look specifically at pages 7–13 and estimate about how many apples and cups of flour to use. *(Adivinen cuántas manzanas y cuántas tazas de harina deben usar.)* Then read to children an apple pie recipe from a cookbook and have them compare it to their answers.

MINI LESSONS

• READING STRATEGY
Retelling Events in Sequence

Using the sentences from pages 3–16 of the book, write each story event on a separate sentence strip. Have children work together in small groups to arrange these events in order, using the book or logic to determine the sequence. Then ask volunteers to retell the events of the story in order. *(Quiero que cuenten el libro en el orden correcto.)*

• LANGUAGE PATTERN
Using Action Words

Ask children to name the action words in the story *(cultivan, recogerlas, llenamos, lavamos, pelamos, cernimos, echamos, amasamos, ponemos, agregamos, medimos, horneamos, comemos)*. Write them on the board. Have children use these words to complete context sentences that you provide. Use sentences such as the following: ____ *la harina*. Although this same sentence is in the book and *cernimos* is used, allow children to choose any word that makes sense.

PHONICS FOCUS

Identifying the Initial and Medial /l/ Sound

Tell children that the /l/ sound is represented by the letter l. *(Vamos a repasar el sonido de la /l/ representado por la letra l.)* Reread the story, pointing out the words *las, lavamos,* and *pelamos* in the book. Write these words on the board. Ask children to think of other words with the /l/ sound in the initial or medial position. *(Piensen en palabras con el sonido /l/.)* Possible answers include *labio, algo, loro,* and *alentar*.

Manzanas y más manzanas

BEFORE READING

Bring in an apple and cut it in half. Help children point out the core, seeds, and stem *(el corazón, las semillas, el tallo)*. Have children share their apple-picking experiences, if any. *(Compartan si han tenido alguna experiencia recogiendo manzanas.)* Then display the nonfiction book and point out the author and title. *(Miren este libro, el nombre del autor y el título.)* Ask children what they think they might learn about in this book. *(¿Qué creen que podrán aprender de este libro?)*

READING

Set a purpose for reading by telling children that they will be reading facts about apples and apple trees. *(Van a leer datos informativos sobre las manzanas y los manzanos.)* Help children recognize that the pictures also provide information. *(Las fotografías también les darán información.)*

Use questions such as these to guide the reading:
- ¿Cómo los ayuda la fotografía en la página 4 a comprender lo que es un huerto?
- ¿Qué es una provincia? ¿Qué claves podrían utilizar para saber el significado de esta palabra?
- ¿En qué formas creen que los recogedores de manzanas pueden llegar a las manzanas que están muy altas en los árboles?

AFTER READING

Discuss *Manzanas y más manzanas*. Ask children to discuss any facts about apples that they learned from the book. *(Hablen de cualquier dato sobre las manzanas que aprendieron del libro.)* Review the children's Before Reading predictions and tell about any fact that surprised them.

Response Activities

States and Provinces
Materials: wall map that shows U.S. and Canada

Explain that the states and provinces referred to in *Manzanas y más manzanas* are in the United States (states) and Canada (provinces). *(Los estados y las provincias están en los Estados Unidos [los estados] y en el Canadá [las provincias].)* Display a map of North America and use yarn to outline the border between these two countries. Then have volunteers take turns pointing to Canada or the United States as you alternate saying *estado* or *provincia*.

MINI LESSONS

• READING STRATEGY
Using Context to Identify Key Words

Ask children, *¿Cómo sabrían ustedes lo que significa la palabra "huertos" en la pagina 4 si no la reconocen?* Have them tell how the meaning of the sentence and the picture clues can help them figure out the word. Have partners take turns reading new words aloud and discussing the clues they used. *(Tomen turnos con su pareja leyendo las palabras nuevas en voz alta y hablando de las claves que usaron para averiguar el significado de estas palabras.)*

• LANGUAGE PATTERN
Modifying Plurals to Singular Forms

Write on the board the following words: *manzanas, huertos, semillas, manzanos, rosas, mercados, comidas,* and *caballos*. Tell children, *Estas palabras significan que son más de una.* Then ask what these words have in common (end with s). *(¿Qué tienen en común estas palabras?) [Todas terminan con s.]* Erase the *s* in each word and have children tell how the meaning of each word changes. *(¿Cómo cambian las palabras?) [Cambia el significado de la palabra.]*

PHONICS FOCUS

Identifying *r* Consonant Blends

Explain to children that some consonants may blend but still retain their own sound. *(Algunas consonantes se unen pero mantienen sus sonidos propios.)* Point out the *r* blends in the book *(crecen, producen, provincias)*. Reread the story with children, having them clap when they hear an *r* consonant blend. Write the words on the board. Call on children to circle each *r* blend.

Tying the Pair Together

Display the two books in this pair. Ask children to point out some similarities and differences between the two books. *(Díganme en qué son parecidos y en qué son diferentes estos dos libros.)* Have children share some facts they have learned about apples. *(Compartan algunos datos que hayan aprendido sobre las manzanas. Digan cómo se recogen las manzanas y cómo se usan.)* Tell them, *Refiéranse a las ilustraciones, las fotografías y el texto en sus charlas.*

Creative Arts: Making Apple Prints
Materials: several apple halves, paint in shallow dishes, aprons

Cut several apples in half and have children dip them in paint and stamp them onto paper to make prints *(hacer huellas)*. Show them how to dig out the seeds and glue them on the paper to make a design in the middle of each print.

Writing: Apple Picking
Materials: writing paper, pencils, drawing paper

Ask children to imagine what it would be like for them to pick apples with their families. If some children have done this, ask them to share their experience with the class. *(Si tienen alguna experiencia en recoger manzanas, compártanla con la clase.)* Then have children write and illustrate a sentence about picking apples with a family member.

Health/Nutrition: Apple Delights
Materials: apples, peanut butter, sesame seeds, raisins

Show children how to prepare a healthful snack, using apples. Core several apples. Then invite children to fill the holes with peanut butter *(mantequilla de maní)* and to sprinkle sesame seeds *(semillas de sésamo)* or raisins *(pasitas)* on top. Let children write the recipe and eat the snack.

ASSESSMENT

- Ask children to tell what they have learned about apples. Record and date these responses.
- Review the objectives given in the lessons for *Pasteles de manzana en familia* and *Manzanas y más manzanas*. Place samples of children's work on these objectives in their portfolios.
- Use informal conferencing with children to assess reading, language, and phonics skills they have learned from the books.

For further assessment ideas and checklists, see pages 78–80.

Home Activities

Copy and distribute to children the *Llévame a casa* activity master found on page 18. Have children ask a family member to help them prepare an apple dish, using a family recipe. Children can copy the recipe and draw a picture of the treat.

Tie It to English

LISTENING/SPEAKING/READING

Forming Phrases

Vocabulary Words/Phrase: *fill, wash, eat, apples, apple pie, baskets*

Go through the book with children, pointing out the vocabulary words and phrase and the illustrations that depict them. Make two columns on the board: one with the action words and one with the naming words. Review the meaning of each word and model pronunciation. Then call on volunteers to pick one word from each column to make a logical phrase *(pick apples, eat apple pie, fill baskets)*.

READING/SPEAKING

Forming Complete Sentences

Distribute copies of the activity below. Have children make up sentences by choosing an illustration or word from each column. *(You eat apple pie.)* Guide children to compose logical sentences. Encourage children to say their sentence aloud as they pantomime the action.

I	fill	(apples)
You	wash	(apple pie)
They	eat	(baskets)

17

LLÉVAME A CASA

Estimada familia de _____,

ACTIVIDADES SOBRE LAS MANZANAS

Su niño ha estado leyendo sobre los productos de manzanas y de cómo éstas crecen. El libro *Pasteles de manzana en familia* es sobre una familia que recoge, lava y pela las manzanas para luego hacer deliciosos pasteles. *Manzanas y más manzanas* es un ensayo fotográfico de cómo crecen las manzanas desde que son semillas y sobre la variedad de productos hechos con manzanas. Ayude a su niño a aprender más sobre las manzanas realizando algunas de las actividades que siguen.

LIBROS ACERCA DE LAS MANZANAS:

Ayude a su niño a aprender más sobre las manzanas llevándolo a visitar la biblioteca. Busquen juntos libros como *La canción del manzano* por Jaroslav Seifert y *El poni, el oso y el manzano* por Sigrid Heuck.

EL CINE, LA MÚSICA Y MÁS:

Vea películas como *The Apple Dumpling Gang* y *Blancanieves* con su niño. Pídale que le explique cómo habría sido diferente la película sin manzanas.

Busque o invente cantos o rimas sobre manzanas o pasteles de manzana para cantar con su niño.

PROYECTO DE ARTE: Pescando manzanas

Materiales: manzanas de diferentes colores, creyones o marcadores, papel, cubo de agua

Llene un cubo con agua y ponga las manzanas adentro. Túrnese con su niño para pescar las manzanas con la boca. Pídale que anote los resultados de la pesca haciendo un dibujo de cada manzana para crear una tabla que muestre los diferentes tipos de manzanas que sacaron del cubo.

PARA COMPARTIR:

Visite un supermercado y agrupe manzanas de diferentes variedades. Ayude a su niño a categorizarlas por color, tamaño o tipo. Pídale que recuerde cómo crecen las manzanas. Parta cada manzana y obsérvenla por dentro. Luego cuenten las semillas. Pídale a su niño que saque algunas conclusiones sobre las semillas de manzana.

INTRODUCING *EN PAREJAS*

Display the covers, pointing out the pictures of the woods. Ask children how the pictures are alike and different. (*¿En qué son las ilustraciones semejantes? ¿En qué son diferentes?*) Write *el bosque* on the chalkboard and invite children to create a word web of things they might see in the woods. (*Hablemos acerca de lo que se puede ver en el bosque.*) Encourage children to discuss stories they know about the woods and trips they may have made to the woods. (*Hablemos sobre cuentos acerca de los bosques y de viajes que hayan hecho a algún bosque.*)

El regreso de Ricitos de Oro

In this version of "Ricitos de Oro," Ricitos returns to the bears' house to find that Osito has made it "Ricitos-proof." Osito has made a successful plan, so he and Cerdita can enjoy their porridge in peace.

Key Words:
preguntó   dijo
gritó   Había una vez

Objectives:
Reading Strategy: Identifying comparisons and contrasts
Language Pattern: Locating dialogue verbs
Phonics Focus: Reviewing the initial /r/ sound

¿Quién vive en el bosque?

A photo essay shows animals who live in the woods, presented in question-and-answer format.

Key Words:
la lechuza   el conejo
el venado   la ardilla listada
el zorro   el oso

Objectives:
Reading Strategy: Recognizing setting
Language Pattern: Identifying naming words
Phonics Focus: Identifying *que, qui* and *gue, gui* combinations

Additional Components:

Audio Cassette Tape: *El regreso de Ricitos de Oro*
                    ¿Quién vive en el bosque?
Writing Masters, pages 73–77

Other Books About Woods and Forests

Los tres osos, Paul Galdone
Osos por ahí, Joanne Ryder
Los secretos del bosque, Michael Gaffney

El regreso de Ricitos de Oro

BEFORE READING

Share with children a classic version of "Ricitos de Oro y los tres ositos." Introduce the retold version. Ask children to look at the cover and predict what they think will happen in this story. *(Miren la cubierta y díganme que creen que ocurrirá.)*

READING

Set a purpose for reading. Ask children to think about how this story is similar or different from the original tale. *(¿Cómo es este cuento semejante o diferente al cuento original?)* Encourage children to think as they read about what Cerdita and Osito are doing. *(A medida que lean piensen en lo que hacen Cerdita y Osito.)*

Use questions such as these to guide the reading:
- ¿Qué tipo de cuento creen que es éste?
- ¿Qué hizo Ricitos de Oro que molestó a Osito?
- ¿Cómo es diferente Osito en este cuento en comparación con el cuento original?

AFTER READING

Talk about *El regreso de Ricitos de Oro*. Ask children if they liked this version as well as the original tale, and why (or why not). *(¿Les gustó esta versión del cuento tanto como el original? ¿Por qué? ¿Por qué no?)* Review children's predictions to see if anyone guessed how the story would turn out.

Response Activities

A Trap for Ricitos de Oro
Materials: string, ice cubes, plastic bugs, a pillow

Display the materials and ask children how Osito and Cerdita might use some of them to keep Ricitos de Oro away. Children can brainstorm suggestions and ideas for new traps, such as rigging a pillow over a door or putting an ice cube in the porridge. Be sure to point out that Osito's tricks were safe, not dangerous to Ricitos de Oro. *(Fíjense que los trucos de Osito no eran peligrosos ni dañinos para Ricitos de Oro.)*

Making Signs
Materials: poster board, markers

Working in pairs, have children write and draw new signs to discourage Ricitos de Oro from coming into Osito's house *(Fuera, No entre, Váyase, No se siente, Mala comida)*. Tell children to be creative with ideas for words and picture messages.

MINI LESSONS

• READING STRATEGY

Identifying Comparisons and Contrasts

Ask how Osito's actions in the story differ from the original tale. *(¿En qué difieren las acciones de Osito del cuento original?)* Discuss what makes this story like the original tale *(los personajes, el problema y el medio ambiente)*. Point out that many fairy tales also contain repetitive language *(lenguaje repetitivo)*. Reread the story and have children chime in on the repeated phrases *Cerdita preguntó* and *Osito dijo*.

• LANGUAGE PATTERN

Locating Dialogue Verbs

Have children brainstorm other words that can be used for *dijo* when reading or writing dialogue. Point out the words *preguntó* and *gritó* in the story. Help children understand that these words tell how the characters said their lines. Ask, *¿Cómo es diferente el significado de estas dos oraciones?* —Limpia tu cuarto —dijo mamá and —Limpia tu cuarto —gritó mamá.

PHONICS FOCUS

Reviewing the Initial /r/ Sound

Read the title of the story to the children, explaining that the initial /r/ sound is like a motor. Demonstrate the sound. *(El sonido /r/ al principio de una palabra suena como un motor en marcha.)* Review with children that this sound is represented by the letter r. *(La letra r representa el sonido inicial /r/.)* As you reread the story to children, have them make the initial /r/ sound when they hear it: *rótulo, regrese, Ricitos, rompió, regreso,* and *ruidosa*.

¿Quién vive en el bosque?

BEFORE READING

Have children think of some animals that live in the woods. *(Piensen en los animales que viven en los bosques.)* Help them decide on animal categories, such as *animales con piel, animales con plumas* and *animales grandes y pequeños*. Write the names in a Venn diagram. Show the cover and read the title. Ask children to predict the answers to the title question.

READING

Set a purpose for reading. Ask children what the text and photographs tell them about where the photo essay takes place. *(¿Qué les dicen el texto y las fotografías sobre dónde sucede el cuento?)* Encourage them to identify the animals and think about where they would add them to the Venn diagram.

Use questions such as these to guide the reading:
- *¿En qué se parece este libro a un paseo por el bosque?*
- *Miren bien las fotos. ¿Cómo creen que se esconde cada animal?*
- *¿Quién es la persona en el cuento? ¿Qué hace esa persona?*

AFTER READING

Ask children what they have learned about the woods and woodland life. *(¿Qué han aprendido sobre el bosque y la vida en el bosque?)* Revisit the riddles in *¿Quién vive en el bosque?* Encourage children to add other clues to the animal riddles that might help a reader figure out the animal names.

Response Activities

Hidden Pictures
Materials: drawing paper, crayons, glue

Have children draw pictures in which they hide as many different animals in the woods as they can. *(Hagan dibujos en los cuales ustedes escondan todos los animales del bosque que puedan.)* Some children may wish to glue pieces of paper over their animals to create flap pictures.

Writing Riddles
Materials: drawing paper, pencils, crayons, markers

Ask children to make up an animal riddle similar to the ones in the story. Have them write the answer on the back of the drawing paper. Suggest they illustrate their riddles and compile them into a class riddle book. *(Decoren sus adivinanzas y pónganlos en un libro para la clase.)*

MINI LESSONS

• READING STRATEGY
Recognizing Setting

Ask children where the photo essay takes place. *(¿En dónde sucede el cuento?)* Ask them how they could tell this even if the title were different. *(¿Si el título del cuento fuera diferente, podrían saberlo igual?)* Discuss how details such as *los árboles, los animales,* and *el guardabosques* tell them this photo essay is set in the woods.

• LANGUAGE PATTERN
Identifying Naming Words

Ask children to look through the book to name some animals that live in the woods (*la lechuza, el conejo, el venado, la ardilla listada, el zorro, el oso*). List each name in a column titled *Animales*. Then ask children to look through the story to find other words that name things (*orejas, piel, cola, nueces*) or places (*bosque, guarida, cueva*). Write these in columns called *Cosas* and *Lugares*.

PHONICS FOCUS

Identifying *que, qui* and *gue, gui* Combinations

On the board write *gue, gui, que,* and *qui,* underlining the letter *u* in all combinations. Explain that the letter *u* is not sounded but is important because it retains the sound of /g/ as in the word *alguien* and the sound of /k/ as in *quién*. Reread the story with children, asking them to form the letter *u* with their thumb and index finger every time you read a word with the *que, qui, gue,* or *gui* combination. *(Formen la letra u cada vez que lean una palabra con las combinaciones que, qui, gue, gui.)*

21

Tying the Pair Together

Ask children what is similar about the books in this pair and what is different. (*¿En qué se parecen este par de libros? ¿En qué son diferentes?*) Have children point out details in the illustrations and photos to show how the woods differ in each story. Help them understand that both books are set in the woods, but that one is based on a traditional tale (*un cuento tradicional*) and one is based on facts (*basado en hechos verdaderos*).

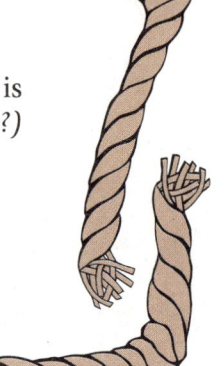

Drama: Ricitos de Oro and Her Friends
Materials: paper plates, art paper, glue, scissors, crayons

Have children create paper-plate masks of Ricitos de Oro, Osito, and Cerdita and other animals who live in the woods. Have them retell their own version of "Ricitos de Oro." (*Cuenten su propia versión de Ricitos de Oro, agregando otros animales que podrían encontrar en el bosque.*) Encourage children to use voices that they think would fit the characters.

Science: Forest Facts
Materials: library books about forests, paper, pencils, art paper, crayons

To learn more about forests, ask children to use books and magazines. (*Usen libros y revistas para aprender más sobre los bosques.*) Have children name some animals and plants that can be found in forests. (*Nombren los animales y las plantas que se encuentran en los bosques.*) Then tell them to write about and draw what they have learned. (*Escriban y dibujen lo que han aprendido.*)

Social Studies: Forest Rangers
Materials: none

Ask children what they think it would be like to be a forest ranger. (*¿Cómo creen que sería ser un guardabosques?*) Explain that forest rangers work to protect our national parks. (*Los guardabosques trabajan para proteger nuestros parques nacionales.*) Have a volunteer role-play a forest ranger. If possible, invite a forest ranger to visit the class.

ASSESSMENT

- Ask children to tell what they have learned about the woods. (*¿Qué han aprendido sobre los bosques?*) Record and date these responses.
- Review the objectives given in the lessons for *El regreso de Ricitos de Oro* and *¿Quién vive en el bosque?* Place samples of children's work on these objectives in their portfolios.
- Use informal conferencing with children to assess reading, language, and phonics skills they have learned from the books.

For further assessment ideas and checklists, see pages 78–80.

Home Activities

Copy and distribute to children the *Llévame a casa* activity master found on page 24. Suggest children go on a walk with a family member to a woods or another outdoor area. They can draw and label a map to show where they walked and then bring the map to share with classmates.

Tie It to English

LISTENING/SPEAKING

Matching Words to Pictures
Vocabulary Words: *owl, rabbit, deer, squirrel, fox, bear*

Bring pictures of the animals in *¿Quién vive en el bosque?* to class. Teach the vocabulary words to children. Then divide the class into two groups. Give one group the pictures of the animals. Give the other group index cards with the animal names on them. Children find their partner by showing their card and asking, *Who has a (fox)?* The child who has the matching card answers, *I have a (fox).*

LISTENING/SPEAKING/WRITING

Understanding and Responding to Questions

Distribute copies of the activity below. Ask children the following question about the first illustration below: *Is the owl in the tree?* Encourage children to answer in complete sentences. (*Yes, the owl is in the tree.*) Have children circle *Yes* or *No* to answer the question. Continue in the same manner, asking the following questions: *Is the fox jumping? Does the rabbit have long ears? Does the deer have one ear?*

---

1. 
Yes   No

2. 
Yes   No

3. 
Yes   No

4. 
Yes   No

23

LLÉVAME A CASA

Estimada familia de _____,

ACTIVIDADES SOBRE LOS BOSQUES

Pídale a su niño que comparta lo que ha leído sobre los bosques. *El regreso de Ricitos de Oro* cuenta como Osito y Cerdita hacen de todo para evitar que Ricitos de Oro regrese a la cabaña de los Osos. *¿Quién vive en el bosque?* es un ensayo fotográfico que muestra los animales que viven en el bosque. Usted puede ayudar a su niño a aprender más sobre los bosques realizando algunas de las actividades que siguen.

LIBROS ACERCA DE LOS BOSQUES:

Ayude a su niño a aprender más sobre los bosques llevándolo a visitar la biblioteca. Busque libros como *Los tres osos* por Paul Galdone, *Osos por ahí* por Joanne Ryder y *Los secretos del bosque* por Michael Gaffney.

EL CINE, LA MÚSICA Y MÁS:

Vean películas que ocurran en el bosque como *Bambi*, *Los tres cerditos*, *Ricitos de Oro y los tres osos* y *La caperucita roja*. Pídale a su niño que genere una lista de todos los animales del bosque que vea.

PROYECTO DE ARTE: Cosas de la naturaleza

Materiales: corteza u hojas, creyones, papel de dibujo, cinta adhesiva, periódicos

Recolecte corteza y hojas con su niño. Arregle la corteza y las hojas en una mesa o en un periódico. Péguelas para sujetarlas. Después pídale a su niño que ponga un papel de dibujo sobre la corteza y las hojas y que frote el lado de un creyón por la superficie del papel.

PARA COMPARTIR:

Camine por un parque o por el vecindario con su niño. Pídale a su niño que lleve un sujetapapeles, papel y un lápiz para anotar o dibujar todos los animales que viven al aire libre. Anime a su niño a recordar aquellos animales sobre los cuales aprendió en *¿Quién vive en el bosque?* (la lechuza, el venado, el zorro, el conejo, la ardillita listada, el oso).

Ayude a su niño a aprender más sobre los hogares de los animales del bosque. Anímelo a crear un diorama del bosque en una caja de zapatos usando piedras, tierra, hojas, ramitas, conos de pino y pasto.

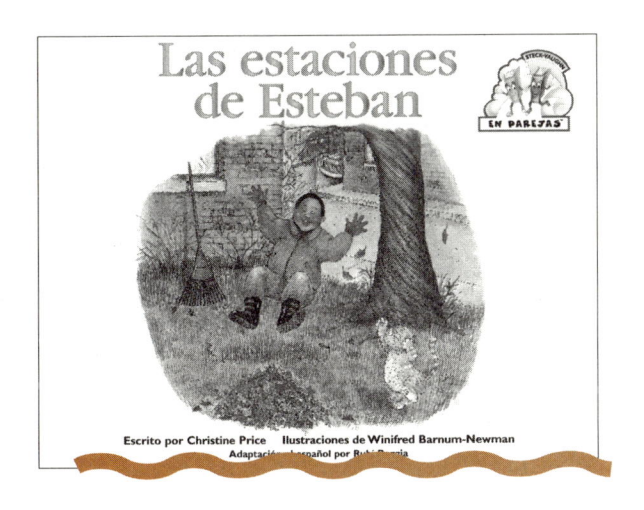

INTRODUCING *EN PAREJAS*

Point out the pictures on each book cover and have children discuss and compare the seasons. *(Vamos a hablar de las estaciones y compararlas.)* Then divide a piece of chart paper into four panels. Write the names of the four seasons, each in a separate panel. Invite children to name the months in each season and to share their favorite seasonal activities. *(Digan los meses en cada estación y compartan cuáles son sus actividades favoritas de cada estación.)* List, date, and initial their responses on the chart.

Las estaciones de Esteban

As Esteban helps his mom search for his missing boots, he recalls the fun he had wearing them throughout the seasons. Esteban finds the boots at last, only to discover that he has outgrown them.

Key Words:

primavera	charcos
mojé	la nieve
trineo	pequeñas
frené	

Objectives:

Reading Strategy: Demonstrating story sequence
Language Pattern: Applying action words
Phonics Focus: Identifying final vowels with accents

Las estaciones del año

This beautiful photo essay shows how plants and animals change throughout the seasons. It ends by indicating the cyclical nature of the seasons.

Key Words:

el verano	el otoño
el invierno	la primavera
las hojas	las comadrejas
los árboles	verdes
duermen	

Objectives:

Reading Strategy: Identifying cause and effect
Language Pattern: Recognizing names of the seasons
Phonics Focus: Identifying the /ñ/ sound

Additional Components:

Audio Cassette Tape: *Las estaciones de Esteban*
Las estaciones del año
Writing Masters, pages 73–77

Other Books About Seasons

El niño que no creía en la primavera, Lucille Clifton, translated by Alma Flor Ada
Las estaciones, John Burningham

Las estaciones de Esteban

BEFORE READING

Display some clothing items that are worn in various seasons, such as *botas, paraguas, guantes,* and *trajes de baño*. Have children identify the items and the seasons in which they are worn. *(Quiero que me digan el nombre de todos los artículos y en qué estación se usan.)* Introduce the book. Ask children to predict what they think will happen in the story. *(¿Qué piensan que ocurrirá en el cuento?)*

READING

Set a purpose for reading. Ask children to think about the order in which Esteban remembers things. *(Piensen en el orden en el cual Esteban recuerda las cosas.)* Encourage them to observe how Esteban's physical appearance changes throughout the story. *(Fíjense como cambia la apariencia de Esteban a través del cuento.)*

Use questions such as these to guide the reading:
- ¿Por qué creen que Esteban no quiere buscar sus botas?
- ¿En qué estación creen que Esteban usó las botas con más frecuencia?
- ¿Cuál era la estación al comienzo del cuento?

AFTER READING

While discussing *Las estaciones de Esteban,* ask children if they were surprised when they read at the end of the story that Esteban's boots no longer fit. *(¿Les sorprendió saber que las botas de Esteban ya no le quedaban bien al final del cuento?)* Review children's pre-reading predictions and discuss whether they proved to be true.

Response Activities

Cassette Tapes
Materials: tape recorder, blank tapes

Encourage children to experiment with their voices to show how Esteban and his mom might sound. Ask, *¿Cómo cambia la voz de la mamá de Esteban cada vez que le pregunta sobre las botas? ¿Cómo cambia la voz de Esteban cada vez que le contesta?* Tape-record pairs of children as they re-enact the story.

Picture Postcards
Materials: unlined index cards, crayons, markers

Have each child choose a favorite season. Tell them to write and draw a postcard from Esteban to his mom, describing what he did in that season. *(Escriban y dibujen una postal de Esteban a su mamá que cuente lo que él hizo en cada estación.)*

MINI LESSONS

• READING STRATEGY
Demonstrating Story Sequence

Ask children to recall the order of the seasons given in the book. In order, have them demonstrate what Esteban did each season, and then explain how the book would have been sequenced if it began with what Esteban did in autumn. *(Expliquen la secuencia del libro si Esteban hubiera comenzado con lo que hizo en el otoño.)*

• LANGUAGE PATTERN
Applying Action Words

Ask children to locate the action words found in the story. Invite volunteers to use these words to play a variation of "Simon Says," using the name *Esteban* in a simple direction such as *Esteban dice, "Recoge las hojas."* Children respond by pantomiming the action word. If they respond when the name *Esteban* is not given, they must sit down.

PHONICS FOCUS

Identifying Final Vowels with Accents

Explain that in this story there are many words that end in a vowel with an accent over it. *(Hay muchas palabras que terminan en una vocal con acento, como mamá, dejé, usé, llovió.)* Create a chart on the board with the headings *á, é, í,* and *ó*. Reread the story and have children raise their hand every time they hear a word that ends in a vowel with an accent. *(Levanten la mano cada vez que oigan una palabra que termine con una vocal con acento.)* Call on volunteers to come to the board and write the word under the correct heading.

LAS ESTACIONES DEL AÑO

BEFORE READING

Post a long strip of paper horizontally at the top of the board and write the seasons of the year across it. Encourage children to think of ways that plants and animals change throughout the seasons. *(Piensen como las plantas y los animales cambian a través de las estaciones.)* List children's ideas under each season name. Introduce the book and ask children to predict what they think will happen. *(Díganme lo que creen que ocurrirá.)*

READING

Set a purpose for reading. Ask children to notice how things change from season to season. *(Fíjense como cambian las cosas de estación a estación.)* Encourage them to listen for any facts that may surprise them. *(Estén pendientes sobre cualquier hecho que los sorprenda.)*

Use questions such as these to guide the reading:
- ¿Qué le ocurre a las plantas en la primavera?
- ¿Cuál es la razón por la cual las hojas cambian de color?
- ¿Qué hacen los animales para mantenerse seguros durante el invierno?

AFTER READING

Talk about *Las estaciones del año*. Have children tell what they have learned about how plants and animals change throughout the seasons. *(¿Qué han aprendido sobre cómo las plantas y los animales cambian durante el año?)* Ask children to share what they now know about the plants and animals that are in the book. *(Compartan lo que saben ahora sobre las plantas y los animales.)* Review the children's predictions and lists, adding new facts that they have learned.

Response Activities

Writing with Color Words
Materials: pencils, art paper, crayons

Call attention to the color words on pages 7, 10, 12, and 15 in the book *(verdes, rojas, doradas, anaranjadas, pardo, blanco)*. Have children point to the colors in the photographs. *(Señalen los colores en las fotografías.)* Then have them use one of these color words to write a sentence about a season. *(Usen una de estas palabras para escribir una oración sobre una de las estaciones.)*

MINI LESSONS

• READING STRATEGY
Identifying Cause and Effect

Point out that sometimes one event, such as a change of season, can cause another event to happen. *(A veces un suceso, como el cambio de las estaciones, puede ser la causa de que ocurra otro suceso.)* Make a chart with columns headed *Causa* and *Efecto*. In the left column, list the seasons. Then have children walk through the story, noting the changes each season brings. List these seasonal changes in the right-hand column.

• LANGUAGE PATTERN
Recognizing Names of the Seasons

Write on chart paper the names of the seasons found in the story. Invite a child to locate and underline the word *invierno* on the paper. Have others do the same for the three remaining season names. Then cut the names apart, shuffle them, ask a child to arrange them in order, beginning this time with summer *(verano)*, and then read them aloud. Repeat the activity, beginning with a different season each time.

PHONICS FOCUS

Identifying the /ñ/ Sound

Write the word *año* on the board, underlining the ñ. Explain to children that the /ñ/ sound is represented by the letter ñ as in the word *año* in the book title. Have children brainstorm words with the /ñ/ sound in the medial position, such as *niño, sueño, riña*, and then write them on the board. Challenge children to think of words with ñ in the initial position *(ñandú, ñame)*.

Tying the Pair Together

Ask children, *¿En qué son estos dos libros semejantes? ¿En qué son diferentes?* Have them tell what they learned about the seasons. *(Díganme qué han aprendido sobre las estaciones.)* Ask them to point out details about each season in the illustrations, photos, and text. *(Señalen detalles de las fotos y el texto acerca de cada estación.)*

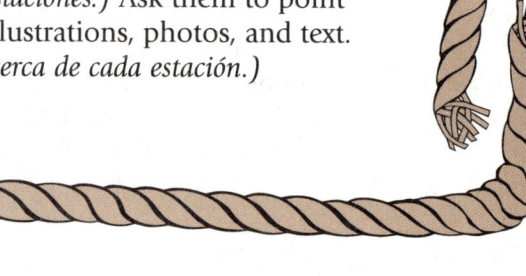

Mathematics: Mark Your Calendars
Materials: blank calendars, art paper, pencils, crayons, glue

Make copies of a blank calendar page and distribute one to each child. Have children complete the calendars by writing in the name of the current month and the weekdays. *(Completen los calendarios escribiendo el nombre del mes y los días de la semana.)* Then tell children to glue these calendars to art paper and illustrate something about the current season.

Science: Weather Map Symbols
Materials: newspaper weather map, art paper, markers, chart paper

Display a prominent weather map from a newspaper. Explain that in a single season, the weather can vary greatly from region to region. *(En una sola estación el tiempo puede variar de región a región.)* Point out the weather symbols, such as raindrops, snowflakes, or smiling suns *(gotas de agua, nieve, soles risueños)*. Have children make some weather map symbols. Each day, ask a volunteer to select the symbol for the current weather condition and post it on a class weather chart.

Gathering Information: Seasonal Things
Materials: pencils, writing paper

Provide for children copies of *Las estaciones de Esteban* and *Las estaciones del año*. Have them work in pairs or small groups to identify and list the seasonal items shown in the illustrations and photos *(hojas, flores, insectos, animales, botas, ropa, juguetes)*.

ASSESSMENT

- Ask children to tell what they have learned about the seasons. *(Díganme qué han aprendido sobre las estaciones.)* Record and date these responses.
- Review the objectives given in the lessons for *Las estaciones de Esteban* and *Las estaciones del año*. Place samples of children's work on these objectives in their portfolios.
- Use informal conferencing with children to assess reading, language, and phonics skills they have learned from the books.

For further assessment ideas and checklists, see pages 78–80.

Home Activities

Copy and distribute to children the *Llévame a casa* activity master found on page 30. Ask children to make lists of things in and around their homes that change from season to season.

Tie It to English

LISTENING/SPEAKING/VIEWING

Identifying Seasons
Vocabulary Words: *season, spring, summer, fall, winter*

Write the word *seasons* on the board, explaining that it means *estaciones*. On the board create four columns, one for each season of the year. Ask children to say words they know in English that they associate with each season *(flowers, plants, snow)*. Write each word in the appropriate column. Have children work on a class mural of the four seasons, making sure the words on the board are incorporated in the mural.

VIEWING/SPEAKING

Talking About the Seasons

Distribute copies of the activity below. Ask children to add an item to each picture, such as a snowman for winter, a rake for fall, and so on. When children are finished, ask them to talk about their drawings and to say what they like about each season.

Winter

Fall

Spring

Summer

LLÉVAME A CASA

Estimada familia de _____,

ACTIVIDADES SOBRE LAS ESTACIONES DEL AÑO

¿Cuál es la estación del año favorita de su niño? Su niño ha estado leyendo libros sobre las estaciones del año. *Las estaciones de Esteban* cuenta sobre un niño que trata de recordar dónde dejó sus botas y cuando las usó durante las cuatro estaciones. Cuando las encuentra, descubre que le quedan pequeñas. *Las estaciones del año* es un ensayo fotográfico que muestra como las plantas y los animales cambian durante las estaciones. Escoja alguna de las actividades de abajo para ayudar a su niño a aprender más sobre las estaciones del año.

LIBROS ACERCA DE LAS ESTACIONES:

Ayude a su niño a aprender más sobre las estaciones del año llevándolo a visitar la biblioteca. Busque libros como *El niño que no creía en la primavera* de Lucille Clifton y *Las estaciones* por John Burningham.

PROYECTO DE ARTE: Tormentas de nieve

Materiales: papel de arte blanco, tijeras, cinta adhesiva

Ayude a su niño a recortar copos de nieve usando el papel de arte. Debe pegarlas en la ventana para crear el efecto de una tormenta de nieve.

EL CINE, LA MÚSICA Y MÁS:

Vea una película con su niño y pídale que identifique durante cuál estación ocurre. Hable sobre la ropa que usan los personajes, adónde viven y qué tiempo hay. Pregúntele a su niño si cree que la estación ha cambiado durante la película.

Busque o invente cantos o rimas sobre el tiempo y las estaciones para cantar con su niño. Una rima podría ser:

> *Florecitas de colores*
> *adornando el campo están.*
> *Nos anuncian que el otoño*
> *ya nos viene a visitar.*

PARA COMPARTIR:

Muéstrele a su niño un álbum de fotografías de familia para que adivine en qué estación fueron tomadas. Su niño debe usar claves como la ropa, el lugar y el tiempo para determinar la estación del año en que fue tomada cada foto. Luego pídale a su niño que categorice las fotos por estación.

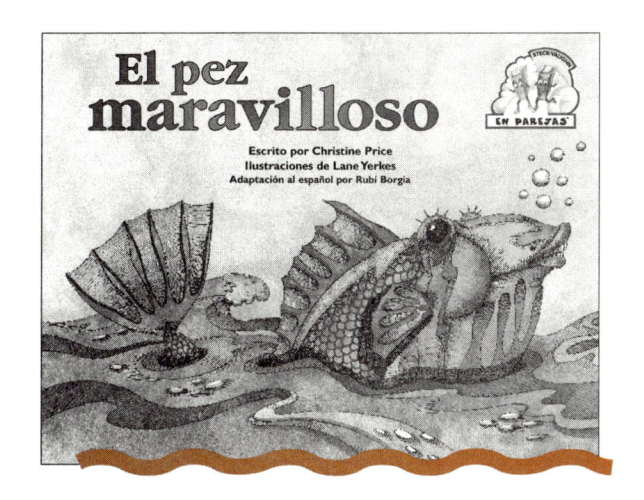

INTRODUCING *EN PAREJAS*

Ask children to share what they know about fish and what they would like to know. *(Hablen de lo que saben de los peces y de lo que quieren saber de ellos.)* Display the two books. Invite children to talk about how the fish on the covers are the same and different. *(Miren los peces en las cubiertas. ¿En qué son semejantes? ¿En qué son diferentes?)* On chart paper write the word *pez.* Ask children to brainstorm facts they know about fish. Focus their brainstorming on what fish are like and how they live *(cómo son los peces y cómo viven).* List, date, and initial their responses. Have children work in small groups to categorize their information, such as *tipos de peces, colores, dónde viven,* and *tamaños.*

El pez maravilloso

A fisherman catches an amazing fish who grants him three wishes. The fisherman asks to be a king and to have a grand castle. When he asks for a bigger castle, the fish denies him. The fisherman wastes his last wish by wishing he had never met the fish. He then meets another amazing fish.

Key Words:
pescador   *pez*
primer   *segundo*
tercer

Objectives:
Reading Strategy: Recalling sequence
Language Pattern: Identifying repetitive dialogue
Phonics Focus: Identifying the /s/ sound in the initial, medial, and final positions

Additional Components:
Audio Cassette Tape: *El pez maravilloso*
Los grandes tiburones blancos
Writing Masters, pages 73–77

Los grandes tiburones blancos

This book compares what children know about themselves to facts about sharks. Presented in a question-and-answer format, the book includes information about how fast a shark can swim, how it swims, and what and how it eats.

Key Words:
grandes   *blancos*
tiburones   *hacia atrás*
hacia adelante

Objectives:
Reading Strategy: Classifying information
Language Pattern: Using question-and-answer format
Phonics Focus: Identifying the /k/ sound before the vowels *a, o,* and *u*

Other Books About Fish
La pesca de Nessa, Nancy Luenn
Los arrecifes de corral, Jenny Wood

31

El pez maravilloso

BEFORE READING

Read aloud a fairy tale or folktale to children. Point out that many fairy tales and folktales begin with *"Había una vez …"* Ask children, *¿Qué les dice esa frase sobre el cuento?* Introduce the book by showing the cover and reading aloud the title. Ask children to predict what they think will happen. *(¿Qué creen que ocurrirá en el cuento?)*

READING

Have children use their predictions to set a purpose for reading. As they read, encourage them to think about what will happen next. *(Piensen en lo que creen que ocurrirá después.)* Help children realize that knowing the story structure of a folktale makes it easier for them to make predictions. *(Cuando saben la estructura de una leyenda, es más fácil predecir lo que ocurrirá.)*

Use questions such as these to guide the reading:
- ¿En qué es diferente este pez a los peces verdaderos?
- ¿Qué hará el pez por el pescador?
- ¿Creen que el pescador pide buenos deseos? Expliquen por qué piensan que sí, o por qué piensan que no.

AFTER READING

Talk about this version of a folktale. Ask children to tell how this story is like other folktales. *(¿En qué forma es este cuento como otras leyendas?)* [tiene un castillo, deseos y comienza con "Había una vez …"] Review children's Before Reading predictions and lead them to discuss whether their predictions proved to be true.

Response Activities

Then What Happened?
Materials: writing paper, pencils, crayons

Remind children that at the end of this story the fisherman catches another amazing fish. *(Recuerden que al final del cuento, el pescador pesca otro pez maravilloso.)* Ask children to write a page telling what they think might happen next. *(Escriban una página que diga lo que piensan ustedes qué podría pasar después.)* Have children illustrate their page.

MINI LESSONS

• READING STRATEGY
Recalling Sequence

Write the following sentences on the board. Have children label them *primero, segundo, tercero.* Check their responses with the book.
El pescador pidió un castillo dorado.
El pescador pidió ser rey.
El pez dijo:—Te concederé tres deseos.

• LANGUAGE PATTERN
Identifying Repetitive Dialogue

Ask children to explain how they know who is talking and what is being said. *(¿Cómo saben quién habla y qué están diciendo?)* Point out how quotation marks help. *(Deben fijarse en los signos ortográficos.)* Ask children to find two pages where the fish and fisherman say similar things (pages 3 and 4). Read these pages with children, emphasizing the repetitive dialogue. Ask children to describe how reading one page helps them read the next one. *(Describan como el leer una página les ayuda a leer la próxima.)*

PHONICS FOCUS

Identifying the /s/ Sound in the Initial, Medial, and Final Positions

Explain to children that the /s/ sound, found at the beginning, the middle, and the end of words, is represented by three letters. *(El sonido /s/ aparece al principio, en el medio y al final de las palabras y es representado por tres letras: s, z, y la c.)* Create a chart with the headings *Posición Inicial, Media,* and *Final* for children to copy. Reread the story, pausing after each page so that children can note in their charts if they heard the initial, medial, or final /s/ sound. *(En sus papeles, marquen el sonido /s/ que oyen.)*

Los grandes TIBURONES blancos

BEFORE READING

Share photos of sharks with children. On the board or on chart paper, label two columns *Lo que sabemos de los tiburones* and *Lo que queremos saber*. Guide children to tell facts and ask questions about sharks. Write their responses in the correct columns. Then have children think about what they can do and what a shark can do. *(Piensen sobre lo que ustedes pueden hacer y lo que un tiburón puede hacer.)* Introduce the book. Ask children to predict what they think will happen in the book. *(¿Qué creen que ocurrirá en el cuento?)*

READING

Have children use their facts and questions to set a purpose for reading. Encourage them to look for answers to their questions as they read.

Use questions such as these to guide the reading:
- ¿En qué se parecen la forma en que ustedes nadan y la forma en que el tiburón nada?
- ¿Qué dato acerca de los tiburones les parece más interesante?
- ¿Cómo se puede aprender más acerca de los tiburones?

AFTER READING

Lead children to talk about this book and the new information they have learned about sharks. Add a third column to the chart from the Before Reading activity: *Lo que aprendimos*. Ask children if anything in the book surprised them. *(¿Hubo algo en el libro que les sorprendió?)* Review their list of pre-reading questions and note how many of their questions were answered.

Response Activities

The Swimming Lesson
Materials: none

Have children demonstrate different swimming styles to the class, such as the crawl *(nadar estilo crol)*, the backstroke *(brazada de espaldas)*, and the dog paddle *(nadar estilo perrito)*. Ask children who know how to swim to tell about how they learned. *(Cuenten cómo aprendieron a nadar.)* Then ask children to guess what a shark's swimming style might be called. *(¿Cómo creen que se llamaría el estilo de natación de un tiburón?)*

MINI LESSONS

- **READING STRATEGY**
  Classifying Information

  Ask children to name facts that they know about sharks. *(Digan algunos datos que conocen sobre los tiburones.)* Then help them classify their information in a web. Write *tiburones* in the center of a circle. Then draw lines extending from the circle. Label the lines *Lo que comen los tiburones*, *Donde viven los tiburones*, and *Tipos de tiburones*. Children can list their information under each heading.

- **LANGUAGE PATTERN**
  Using Question-and-Answer Format

  Point out the question marks and the periods in the text. Reread the text with children, pointing out the question-and-answer format. As a class, create a short question and answer book about pets, using *Los grandes tiburones blancos* as a model for writing.

PHONICS FOCUS

Identifying the /k/ Sound Before the Vowels *a*, *o*, and *u*

Explain to children that the letter *c*, used before the vowels *a*, *o*, and *u*, represents the /k/ sound. *(La letra c representa el sonido /k/ antes de las vocales a, o y u.)* As you reread the story, tell children to listen for the /k/ sound. *(Escuchen el sonido /k/ mientras leo.)* Write these words on the board: *blanca*, *boca*, *comes*, and *cuna*. Ask volunteers to come to the board, circle the letter *c*, and underline the vowel following it. *(Lean las palabras, hagan un círculo alrededor de la letra c y subrayen la vocal que le sigue.)*

33

Tying the Pair Together

Ask children to tell how the books are the same and different. *(Díganme en qué son semejantes y en qué son diferentes estos dos libros.)* Have them share what they have learned about fish. Invite them to point out details about sharks and other fish in the illustrations, photos, and text. *(Señalen detalles en las ilustraciones, las fotos y el texto acerca de los tiburones y otros peces.)*

Writing: A Fishy Tale
Materials: writing paper, pencils, crayons

Guide children to write a fish story. It could be about a time they went fishing, a pet fish, or an imaginative tale about an amazing shark. *(Escriban un cuento sobre la pesca, sobre un pez mascota o un cuento imaginario sobre un tiburón maravilloso.)* Let children illustrate their stories and then read them to the class.

Mathematics/Creative Arts: Bigger and Smaller Than Me
Materials: art paper, butcher paper, markers, crayons

On art paper have pairs of children draw two fish that are smaller than themselves. Encourage them to make these fish very different in size. *(Dibujen dos peces que sean más pequeños que ustedes. Los peces deben ser diferentes en sus tamaños.)* Then have each pair use butcher paper to draw a fish bigger than themselves. *(Ahora dibujen un pez más grande que ustedes.)* Have them compare their drawings and arrange the drawings by size.

Science/Social Studies: Sea Creature Homes
Materials: none

Many different creatures live in the sea. Ask children to name sea homes, such as shells, water, or caves. *(Nombren algunos hogares del mar como los caracoles, el agua o las cuevas.)* Lead children in a discussion to compare these homes to their own homes.

ASSESSMENT

- Ask children to tell what they have learned about fish. *(Díganme qué han aprendido sobre los peces.)* Record and date these responses.
- Review the objectives given in the lessons for *El pez maravilloso* and *Los grandes tiburones blancos*. Place samples of children's work on these objectives in their portfolios.
- Use informal conferencing with children to assess reading, language, and phonics skills they have learned from the books.

For further assessment ideas and checklists, see pages 78–80.

Home Activities

Copy and distribute to children the *Llévame a casa* activity master found on page 36. Tell children that they will be interviewing their parents about fish. Brainstorm with children a list of questions they might want to ask about fish and fishing.

Tie It to English

LISTENING/SPEAKING

Expressing Wishes

Vocabulary Words/Phrases: *a wish, once upon a time*

Write on the board the words *un deseo*. Next to them write *a wish*. Say the words, explain them, and have children repeat after you. Gather children in a circle. Tell them they will all have a chance to make a wish. Then begin by modeling, "Once upon a time, (your name) had a wish. (He/She) wished for __." The child to your right then repeats, adding what he or she wishes for. Continue like that until all children have made a wish.

LISTENING/SPEAKING

Practicing Pronunciation Through Rhyme

Distribute copies of the activity below. Teach the following traditional rhyme to children. Encourage them to add their wish to the last line.

Star light, star bright,

I wish I may, I wish I might

Have the wish I wish tonight.

My wish is _____.

35

LLÉVAME A CASA

Estimada familia de _____,

ACTIVIDADES SOBRE LOS PECES

¡Chas! ¡Chas! ¡Chas! ¡Glub! ¡Glub! ¡Glub! Su niño ha estado leyendo cuentos sobre los peces. *El pez maravilloso* es acerca de un pez que le concede tres deseos a un pescador. *Los grandes tiburones blancos* cuenta lo que comen los tiburones, cómo nadan y cómo cazan su comida. Para ayudar a su niño a aprender más sobre los peces, escoja alguna de las actividades que siguen.

LIBROS ACERCA DE LOS PECES:

Ayude a su niño a aprender más sobre los peces llevándolo a visitar la biblioteca. Busque libros como *La pesca de Nessa* por Nancy Luenn y *Los arrecifes de corral* por Jenny Wood.

EL CINE, LA MÚSICA Y MÁS:

Vean películas como *The Magic Fish* o *The Little Mermaid*. Hable con su hijo sobre los peces, cómo viven y cómo son representados en las películas.

Busque cantos y rimas sobre los peces o sobre el agua para cantar con su niño. Por ejemplo:

Pececito, pececito
en el agua del claro lago
te veo nadar.
Pececito, pececito
si yo pudiera nadar
¡contigo me gustaría jugar!

PROYECTO DE ARTE: Peces maravillosos

Materiales: papel de arte de color, tijeras, lápiz, pegamento

Invite a su niño a dibujar y luego recortar el contorno de un pez. Use el papel de arte de colores para hacer pedazos circulares de diferentes tamaños. Pídale a su niño que le pegue los papeles circulares al pez para representar las escamas. Exhiba el pez donde la familia lo pueda disfrutar.

PARA COMPARTIR:

Anime a su niño a que le cuente algo sobre los tiburones. Juntos dibujen un tiburón que esté haciendo algo especial como nadando, comiendo o saltando.

INTRODUCING *EN PAREJAS*

Ask children to recall the last time they saw the moon and to tell about their observations. *(¿Cuándo fue la última vez que vieron la luna? ¿Qué pensaron cuando la vieron?)* Then display the two books in this pair, and invite children to discuss how the illustration of the moon compares to the photograph. *(Comparen la ilustración de la luna con la fotografía.)* Ask which one looks most like the moon they are familiar with, and invite children to share any other facts they may know about the moon. *(¿Cuál de ellas se parece más a la luna que ustedes conocen?)*

La luna adormecedora

In rhyming verse, this story describes a sleepy town at nightfall and how the animals and people are lulled to sleep.

Key Words:
claridad   suavidad
tranquilidad oscuridad
luna   brillan
canción de cuna

Objectives:
Reading Strategy: Making inferences about characters
Language Pattern: Recognizing rhyming words
Phonics Focus: Understanding rhyme

El hombre en la Luna

This photo essay relates facts about the moon to things with which children are familiar, and is presented in a question-and-answer format.

Key Words:
queso   agujeros
piensas   brilla
aumenta   disminuye

Objectives:
Reading Strategy: Distinguishing between fact and fiction
Language Pattern: Using question-and-answer format
Phonics Focus: Identifying questioning intonation

Additional Components:

Audio Cassette Tape: *La luna adormecedora*
                    El hombre en la Luna
Writing Masters, pages 73–77

Other Books About the Moon

El ratón que quería comerse la luna, Laura Devetach
El lago de la luna, Iván Gantschev
    translated by Guillermo Gutiérrez

La luna adormecedora

BEFORE READING

Share with children a traditional lullaby such as *"Canción de cuna"* (see Response Activity below). Point out the rhyming and repeating lines and explain that these simulate the repetitive, rocking motion that helps babies fall asleep. *(Las rimas y las líneas repetitivas simulan los movimientos de una cuna que ayudan a que los bebés se duerman.)* Introduce the book. Ask, *¿Qué creen que ocurrirá en el cuento?*

READING

Set a purpose for reading by asking children to pay attention to the people in the story. *(Pónganle atención a los personajes en el cuento.)* Have children think about who the characters are and what they do. Help them see that the words and pictures together tell about the characters.

Use questions such as these to guide the reading:
- *¿Qué hora es en el cuento? ¿Cómo lo saben?*
- *¿Qué personaje es el favorito de ustedes? Expliquen.*
- *Nombren algunos animales que duermen de noche.*

AFTER READING

Talk about *La luna adormecedora*. Ask children how this story is similar to the lullaby *"Canción de cuna"* (both are lullabies, both have rhyming words, both feature babies). *(¿En qué se parece este cuento a la canción de cuna?)* [ambas son canciones de cuna, ambas tienen palabras que riman, ambas se enfocan en los bebés] Review the children's Before Reading predictions.

Response Activities

Traditional Rhyme "Canción de cuna"
Materials: none

Teach children the following lullabye:

El niñito está dormido, la madre cantando va mientras lo mece en la cuna, tralalá, lalá, lalá. Duerme, duerme mi niñito, al lado de tu mamá que todo el mundo te canta, tralalá, lalá, lalá.

Writing about Nighttime
Materials: art paper, markers, scissors, string

Have each child cut out a moon shape and print his or her name on it. On the paper moon, have them write a sentence about nighttime. *(Escriban sobre la luna una oración que diga lo que más les gusta de la noche.)* Attach string to the finished moons and hang them from the ceiling.

MINI LESSONS

• READING STRATEGY
Making Inferences About Characters

Write the characters' names as column heads on the board: *Mami, Papi, la bebita*. Ask children to use the words and picture clues in the book to describe what they think each character is like. *(Utilicen las claves en el cuento para describir a cada uno de los personajes.)* Write their responses in the correct columns. Have children discuss whether they agree with these character descriptions. *(¿Están de acuerdo con estas descripciones de los personajes?)*

• LANGUAGE PATTERN
Recognizing Rhyming Words

Reread pages 2 and 3, emphasizing the words *claridad* and *suavidad*. Ask children to describe where the rhyming words are in the sentences. *(¿Dónde están las palabras que riman en las oraciones?)* [al final] Have children name other rhyming words in the story and discuss their sounds and spellings.

PHONICS FOCUS

Understanding Rhyme

Explain that the rhyme in this story is created by words that have the same final sound. *(La rima en este cuento está creada por palabras que tienen el mismo sonido al final.)* Reread the story, pausing at the end of pages 2, 3, 12, 13, 14, and 15. Ask children to raise their hand when they hear two endings that rhyme. *(Levanten la mano cada vez que oigan dos finales que riman.)* On the board write the pairs of rhyming words: *claridad-suavidad, tranquilidad-oscuridad, ruido-dormido*. Ask children to read each pair of words.

El hombre en la Luna

BEFORE READING

Read aloud the title of the book and ask children, *Do you think there is a man in the moon?* *(¿Creen que hay un hombre en la Luna?)* Tell them that this book asks and answers questions such as this about the moon. *(Este libro hace preguntas y responde a preguntas como éstas sobre la Luna.)* Ask children what questions they think will be included in the book. *(¿Qué preguntas creen que se incluirán en el libro?)*

READING

To set a purpose for reading, have children think about the questions being posed in the story and how someone might answer them. *(Piensen en las preguntas que se hacen en el libro y cómo alguien las podría contestar.)* Help children recognize the difference between fact and opinion.

Use questions such as these to guide the reading:
- *¿Creen que la idea de que la Luna está hecha de queso es un dato verdadero o una opinión?*
- *¿De verdad hay montañas en la Luna? ¿Cómo lo saben?*
- *Basándonos en estos datos, ¿por qué piensan que no hay vida en la Luna?*

AFTER READING

Discuss *El hombre en la Luna*. Ask children to tell what they have learned about the moon from this informational book. *(¿Qué han aprendido sobre la Luna en este libro?)* Discuss the photographs with children and have them point out anything that was surprising. *(Señalen cualquier cosa que encontraron sorprendente.)*

Response Activities

Come Out, Moon
Materials: none

Assign one child to be "la Luna." Ask others to pretend that they are doing a nighttime activity, such as taking a bath or putting on pajamas. Have "la Luna" walk slowly across the room while others pretend to go to sleep. When "la Luna" is finished crossing the room, tell children to pretend to be waking up in the morning.

Moon Art
Materials: art paper, pencils, crayons

Have children illustrate their favorite fact about the moon, using the book for reference or for writing a different fact. *(Dibujen su dato favorito sobre la Luna. Utilicen el libro como referencia o escriban un dato diferente.)* Then ask them to tell about their moon fact. *(Hablen de su dato acerca de la Luna.)*

MINI LESSONS

• READING STRATEGY
Distinguishing Between Fact and Fiction

Create a chart with two columns headed *Datos verdaderos* and *Opiniones*. Walk through the book, asking children to decide whether each question or statement is based on something real *(un dato verdadero)* or an opinion *(una opinión)*. Write their responses in the columns. Point out that the main difference between the two categories is that facts can be proven, but opinions cannot. *(Los datos verdaderos se pueden probar. Las opiniones no se pueden probar.)*

• LANGUAGE PATTERN
Using Question-and-Answer Format

Reread aloud pages 7 and 8. Say, *Describan lo que ven al principio y al final de las palabras en la página 7.* [signos de interrogación] *Ahora describan lo que ven al final de las palabras en la página 8.* [punto final] Have each child write a question about the moon and insert the beginning and ending question marks. Then have children write a sentence that answers the question, ending it with a period.

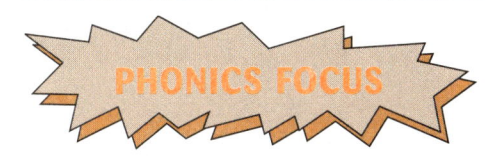

PHONICS FOCUS

Identifying Questioning Intonation

On page 2 read the question, using the correct intonation. Ask children, *¿Fue esa una pregunta o una declaración?* Alternate questions with statements and have children identify the correct questioning intonation. Write questions on the board without the question marks. Call on children to write in the question marks and read the sentences with the proper intonation.

Tying the Pair Together

As you display the two books, remind children of the theme, and have them discuss some similarities *(semejanzas)* and differences *(diferencias)* between the two. Invite children to tell what they have learned about the moon and about what it looks like, referring to the text, illustrations, and photographs. *(Dirigiéndose al texto, las ilustraciones y las fotografías, ¿qué han aprendido sobre la Luna y el aspecto que tiene?)*

Science: Phases of the Moon
Materials: white, black, and dark blue art paper, scissors, glue, pencils

Point out the phases of the moon shown on page 11 of *El hombre en la Luna*. On white art paper, have children draw these phases and label them. Then have children cut them out and glue them onto black or dark blue art paper to show the phases of the moon against a night sky. *(Recorten las fases de la Luna y péguenlas a un papel negro o azul oscuro.)*

Creative Arts: Crayon Resist Moons
Materials: crayons, blue and purple paint, paint brushes, art paper

Have children use crayons to draw nighttime pictures of the moon and stars, bearing down hard to leave a heavy wax coating. Have them use bright or pale colors for the moon and stars. They can then paint over the crayon with blue and purple paint.

Geography: Day and Night
Materials: globe

Display a globe and have children point out where they live. Turn off the classroom lights and shine a flashlight on North America. Help children see that when the light shines on one side of the globe, the other side is dark. *(Cuando la luz brilla en un lado del globo, el otro lado está oscuro.)* Explain that when it is daytime here, it is nighttime on the opposite side of the world.

ASSESSMENT

- Ask children to tell what they have learned about the moon. *(Díganme qué han aprendido sobre la Luna.)* Record and date these responses.
- Review the objectives given in the lessons for *La luna adormecedora* and *El hombre en la Luna*. Place samples of children's work on these objectives in their portfolios.
- Use informal conferencing with children to assess reading, language, and phonics skills they have learned from the books.

For further assessment ideas and checklists, see pages 78–80.

Home Activities

Copy and distribute to children the *Llévame a casa* activity master found on page 42. Tell children that they will be selecting a favorite bedtime story from home, reading it with a family member, and retelling it to the class.

Tie It to English

LISTENING/SPEAKING/VIEWING/WRITING

Identifying Content Area Vocabulary

Vocabulary Words: *moon, Earth, mountains, valleys, air, water*

Write the vocabulary words on the board and explain the meaning of each word. Call on volunteers to look through *El hombre en la Luna* to find the Spanish equivalent of each word. Encourage children to draw a picture that includes the moon, Earth, mountains, a valley, and water. Have children label each of the items pictured.

VIEWING/SPEAKING

A Language Experience Story

Distribute copies of the activity below. Explain to children that they will be writing a story in English about the picture. Invite children to talk about the illustration as you write their comments on the board. Assist with new vocabulary. When children are finished, have volunteers read the comments on the board.

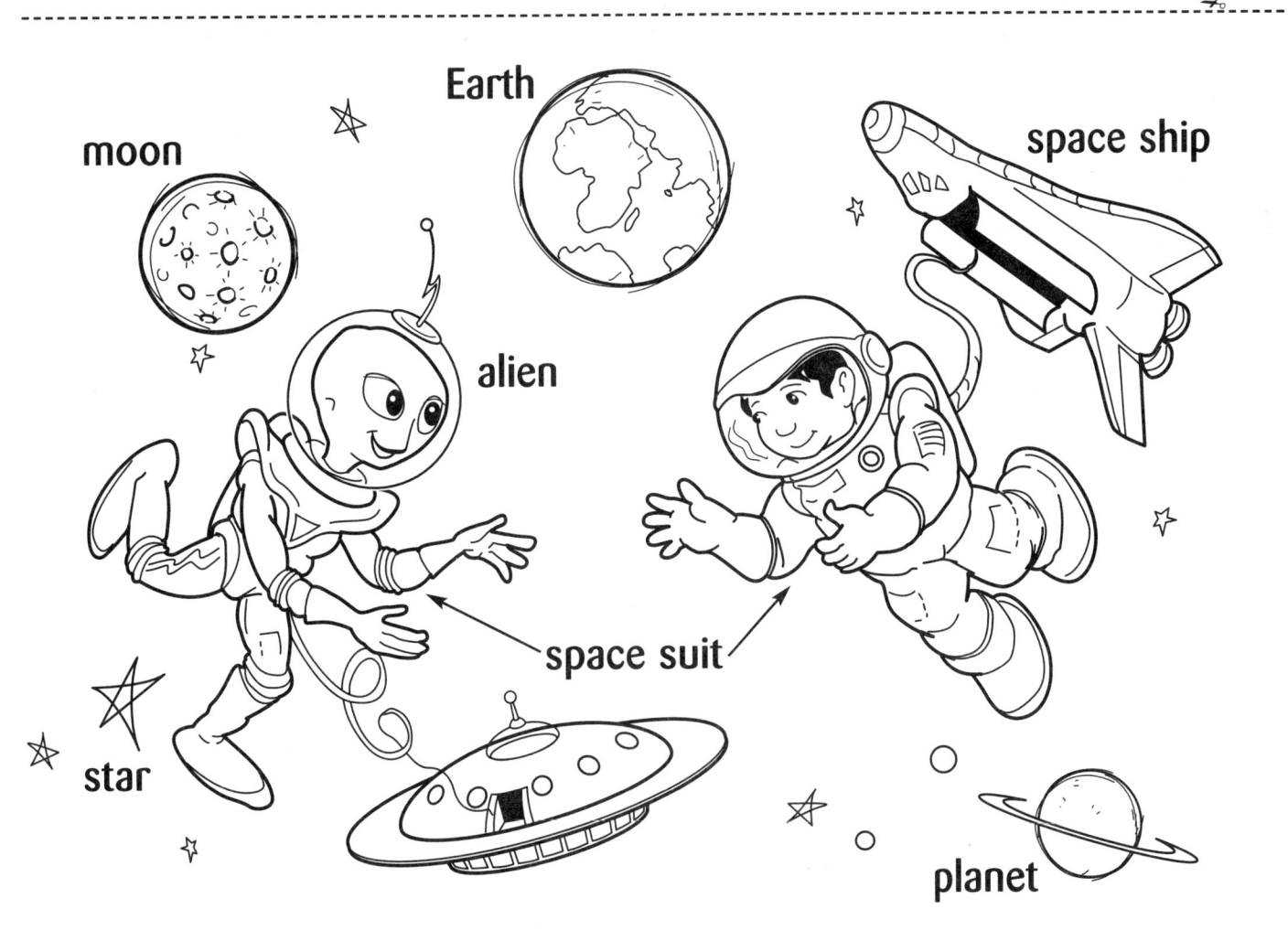

Labeled illustration: moon, Earth, space ship, alien, space suit, star, planet

LLÉVAME A CASA

Estimada familia de _____,

ACTIVIDADES SOBRE LA LUNA

¿Qué hace su familia cuando es hora de acostarse? Su niño ha estado leyendo sobre la Luna y sobre las rutinas de las personas antes de acostarse. *La luna adormecedora* describe un pueblo soñoliento al anochecer y como los padres mecen a sus bebés para que se duerman. *El hombre en la Luna* contesta preguntas básicas sobre la Luna. Ayude a su niño a aprender más sobre la Luna y sobre las rutinas de la hora de acostarse realizando algunas de las actividades que siguen.

LIBROS ACERCA DE LA LUNA:

Ayude a su niño a leer y a aprender más sobre la Luna llevándolo a la biblioteca. Busque libros como *El ratón que quería comerse la luna* por Laura Devetach y *El lago de la luna* por Iván Gantschev.

EL CINE, LA MÚSICA Y MÁS:

Vea películas sobre viajes espaciales, como *Space Camp* o *E.T.* Vea la película con su niño e indíquele las partes donde muestran la Luna. Juntos, repasen los datos que saben sobre la Luna.

Busque cantos o rimas sobre la Luna para compartir con su niño.

PROYECTO DE ARTE: La Luna y las estrellas

Materiales: tijeras, papel de color con adhesivo al reverso, cartulina

Ayude a su niño a hacer un dibujo de una escena del cielo de noche. Pídale que dibuje una Luna grande y muchas estrellas pequeñas en el papel con adhesivo al reverso. Juntos recorten estas formas y péguenlas en la cartulina. Luego pueden dibujar otras cosas como casas, árboles, etc.

PARA COMPARTIR:

Pídale a su niño que haga una encuesta sobre las costumbres a la hora de dormir de la familia. Anímelo a recordar lo que hicieron los personajes en *La luna adormecedora* antes de irse a dormir.

Copyright © Steck-Vaughn Company. All rights reserved.

INTRODUCING *EN PAREJAS*

Ask children to recall a time when they visited a beach or to describe beach pictures they have seen. *(Piensen en alguna vez que hayan ido a la playa o describan alguna fotografía de la playa que hayan visto.)* Refer to a map to point out the coastal areas. Then display the two book covers and help children understand that the photograph on the cover of *Criaturas de la playa* is of a jellyfish *(medusa)* that might be found on or near a beach like the one illustrated on the cover of *El concurso de castillos de arena*.

El concurso de castillos de arena

Excitement builds on Playa Arenosa as the judges try to decide who will win the prize for the best sand castle. A big wave washes all sand castles away but the smallest and simplest of all.

Key Words:

mediano   grande
pequeño   ancho
alto   estrecho

Objectives:

Reading Strategy: Demonstrating how pictures tell a story
Language Pattern: Using describing words
Phonics Focus: Identifying words with four syllables

Criaturas de la playa

Photographs and engaging riddles about small sea animals provide the format for this interactive photo essay.

Key Words:

erizo de mar   estrella de mar
pez sierra   ostra
caballito de mar   medusa

Objectives:

Reading Strategy: Defining key words using context clues
Language Pattern: Separating compound words
Phonics Focus: Identifying the /pl/ sound

Additional Components:

Big Books: *El concurso de castillos de arena*
           Criaturas de la playa
Audio Cassette Tape: *El concurso de castillos de arena*
           Criaturas de la playa
Writing Masters, pages 73–77

Other Books About Beaches

El duende del mar, Hilda Perera
El pescador, Fiona Moodie
El amigo que vino del mar, Mariano Vara

43

El concurso de castillos de arena

BEFORE READING

Ask children how they would build a sand castle. (*¿Cómo harían un castillo de arena?*) Have them discuss experiences they have had with sand and beaches. If a sandy area to play is available, allow groups of children to build small sand castles. Introduce the book. Ask children to predict what they think will happen. (*¿Qué creen que ocurrirá en el cuento?*)

READING

To set a purpose for reading, tell children to pay attention to the details in the illustrations in *El concurso de castillos de arena*. (*Presten atención a los detalles del cuento.*) Tell them to notice what the children in the background are doing. (*Fíjense en lo que hacen los niños que se ven en el fondo de las ilustraciones.*) Help them see that the pictures help tell the story, and that they often provide information that may not be in the text.

Use questions such as these to guide the reading:
- *¿Qué hacen los niños en el fondo de las ilustraciones?*
- *¿Qué llevan los salvavidas por el cuello? ¿Por qué los llevan?*
- *¿Qué familia creen que debe ganar?*

AFTER READING

Talk about *El concurso de castillos de arena*. Ask children how the sand castles in the story compare to ones they have made or seen. (*¿Cómo pueden comparar los castillos de arena en el cuento con los castillos de arena que ustedes conocen?*) Discuss what happened with the wave. (*Díganme qué ocurrió con la ola.*) Review children's Before Reading predictions and discuss how closely they match the story.

Response Activities

Giving Awards
Materials: yellow and blue art paper, scissors, glue, markers

Ask pairs of children to imagine that they are the two lifeguards in the story. Lead them to discuss different awards they might give. (*Imagínense que son los dos salvavidas en el cuento y que tienen que otorgar premios por los castillos de arena, tales como el más alto o el más elegante.*) Have them print the categories on circles of yellow paper and attach two blue paper ribbons to each circle.

Newspaper Headlines
Materials: writing paper, pencils, crayons, markers

Have children write newspaper headlines about the sand castle contest at Playa Arenosa. Suggest they add a picture of one of the castles and a brief caption. (*Hagan un dibujo de uno de los castillos y escriban algo sobre él.*)

MINI LESSONS

- **READING STRATEGY**

Demonstrating How Pictures Tell a Story

Have children look at the illustration on page 14 and tell what they see. (*¿Qué ven en la página 14? [una ola] Lean la página 16 y díganme qué castillo ganó el premio.*) Point out that while the wave and the winning sand castle are not mentioned in the text, they are important events in the story. (*Aunque en el texto no se mencionan la ola y el castillo que ganó el premio, son sucesos importantes en el cuento.*) Cover the text in the story and have children retell the story, using the illustrations.

- **LANGUAGE PATTERN**

Using Describing Words

Ask children to find in the story words that describe the various sizes of the sand castles (*pequeño, mediano, grande, ancho, alto, estrecho*). List the words on the board and have children brainstorm other size words the author could have used, such as *enorme* or *chiquito*. Have children copy the following sentence, adding the size word of their choice: *Yo haría un castillo de arena _____.*

PHONICS FOCUS

Identifying Words with Four Syllables

Review with children that words are formed by syllables and each syllable must contain a vowel sound. (*Las palabras están formadas por sílabas y las sílabas deben tener una vocal.*) On the board copy the words on page 2 and divide them into syllables. Ask the class to read the words with you, tapping on their desk each time they sound out a syllable. (*Lean conmigo, separando las palabras en sílabas tocando los pupitres con sus nudillos.*)

Criaturas de la playa

BEFORE READING

Display a variety of seashells or pictures of shells. Lead children to discuss what they know about shells, animals that live in shells, and where shells can be found. *(Díganme qué saben sobre los caracoles, los animales que viven en los caracoles y dónde se encuentran los caracoles.)* Begin a chart to list children's responses for What We Know *(Lo que sabemos)* and What We Want to Know *(Lo que queremos saber)*. Introduce the book, and ask children to predict the creatures that they think will be in the book. *(¿Qué criaturas creen que habrán en el libro?)*

READING

Set a purpose for reading by telling children that they will be using word clues and picture clues to answer riddles about creatures that live on or near the beach. *(Van a usar claves en las palabras y fotografías para poder descifrar las adivinanzas sobre las criaturas que viven en o cerca de la playa.)*

Use questions such as these to guide the reading:
- ¿Qué es una cierra? ¿Cómo los ayuda la foto y el texto a saberlo?
- ¿Qué quiere decir "hay un tesoro escondido dentro de una ostra"?
- ¿Como los ayudan las adivinanzas a saber las respuestas?

AFTER READING

Invite children to discuss what they have learned about beach creatures from this interactive photo essay. *(Díganme qué han aprendido sobre las criaturas de la playa.)* Add their responses to the chart begun in the Before Reading activity. Ask, *¿Cuántas adivinanzas pudieron contestar correctamente? ¿Tuvieron dificultad en contestarlas?*

Response Activities

Shell Riddles
Materials: shells, drawing paper, markers, crayons

Display the shells from the Before Reading activity. Have children make up riddles about the shells, using the language pattern of the book as a starting point. *(Van a escribir sus propias adivinanzas, usando el mismo patrón del libro.)* When children have illustrated their shell riddles, have them take turns saying their riddles aloud as others guess the answers.

Fishy Names
Materials: drawing paper, crayons, markers, fish books

Write the following names of fish on the board: *pez cebra, pez luna, pez martillo, pez mujer y pez mariposa*. Invite children to draw funny pictures of how they think these fish might look. *(Hagan dibujos cómicos de cómo creen que lucen estos peces.)* Then have them find the fish in a reference book and compare their pictures to the photographs.

MINI LESSONS

• READING STRATEGY
Defining Key Words Using Context Clues

Ask children how they might figure out the meaning of the word *ostra* from the sentence and the photo on page 10. Lead them to see that they could use the photo and the language pattern in the book to figure out that an oyster is a sea creature. *(La foto y el texto les dan la clave que es una ostra.)* In a similar way, help children discuss how they figured out other unfamiliar words in the story *(criaturas, estrella de mar, pez sierra, medusa, caballito de mar)*.

• LANGUAGE PATTERN
Separating Compound Words

Write on the board the compound words *(palabras compuestas)* from the book: *erizo de mar, estrella de mar, pez sierra, caballito de mar*. Ask volunteers to read each of the words aloud. Lead them to understand how the meaning of these words change when they are used together and separately.

PHONICS FOCUS

Identifying the /pl/ Sound

Explain to children that two words in this story begin with the /pl/ sound. *(Dos palabras en este libro comienzan con el sonido /pl/.)* Explain that the /pl/ sound is represented by the letters *p* and *l*. Write the cluster on the board. Reread the story and ask children to clap their hands every time they hear this sound. *(Den una palmada cada vez que oigan el sonido /pl/.)* Encourage children to think of other words with the initial /pl/ sound *(placer, pleno, pluma)*.

45

Tying the Pair Together

Ask children to compare the two books and to support their comparisons by pointing out details. *(Comparen los dos libros, fijándose en los detalles de las fotografías, el texto y las ilustraciones.)* Help them notice that one book takes place on the beach, while the other includes animals that live on the beach or in the ocean. *(La acción de uno de los libros sucede en de la playa mientras que el otro incluye animales que viven en la playa o en el mar.)*

Health: Safety at the Beach
Materials: writing paper, pencils

Have children look through the illustrations and photos in this theme to get ideas for safety at the beach. Discuss the reasons why it is important to protect oneself in the water and sun. *(Díganme por qué es importante protegerse en el agua y del sol.)* Then have children write a list of safety items they might take on a beach trip. *(Escriban una lista de artículos para protección que podrían llevar a la playa: loción protectora del sol, sombreros, zapatos, aletas para nadar.)*

Creative Arts: Sand Paintings
Materials: paints, sand, art paper

Invite children to create paintings of the beach. Then demonstrate how they can add texture to their painting by sprinkling sand onto the painting before it dries. Children may enjoy using sand to separate the foreground, horizon, and background in their paintings.

Music: Making Maracas from Sand
Materials: a 1-cup milk carton for each child, sand, glue, art paper, markers

To make maracas, have children put some sand in a small empty milk carton, seal it completely, and decorate with art paper and markers. Have them play along as they listen to the songs "Allá en la playa" or "Guantanamera."

ASSESSMENT

- Ask children to tell what they have learned about the beach. *(Díganme qué han aprendido sobre la playa.)* Record and date these responses.
- Review the objectives given in the lessons for *El concurso de castillos de arena* and *Criaturas de la playa*. Place samples of children's work on these objectives in their portfolios.
- Use informal conferencing with children to assess reading, language, and phonics skills they have learned from the books.

For further assessment ideas and checklists, see pages 78–80.

Home Activities

Copy and distribute to children the *Llévame a casa* activity master found on page 48. Tell children to share with family members what they have learned about beaches. *(Compartan con sus familias lo que han aprendido sobre la playa.)* Encourage them to ask family members if they have visited a beach and what it was like. *(Pregúntenle a sus familias si han ido a la playa alguna vez y cómo fue esa experiencia.)*

Tie It to English

LISTENING/SPEAKING

Matching Written Language to Pictures
Vocabulary Words/Phrase: *beach, ocean, shovel, pail, ice chest, whistle, sunglasses*

Write the vocabulary words and phrase on index cards. Go through *El concurso de castillos de arena* with children, pointing out the illustrations that depict each of the words as you model pronunciation. Display pictures of the objects named in the vocabulary list above and invite children to match each word card to its picture. Then have children make their own cards, each with a vocabulary word on one side and its illustration on the other.

VIEWING/WRITING/SPEAKING

Distribute copies of the activity below. Have children connect the dots to complete each item. As they complete each one, have children write the name of the item in the space provided. Encourage children to show how to use each item (dig with the shovel, carry the pail, and so on).

47

LLÉVAME A CASA

Estimada familia de _____,

ACTIVIDADES SOBRE LA PLAYA

Su niño ha estado visitando playas imaginarias en sus lecturas. El cuento *El concurso de castillos de arena* cuenta sobre unos niños que ganan el premio por haber construido el mejor castillo de arena. *Criaturas de la playa* reta a los niños a resolver adivinanzas sobre pequeños animales de mar. Ayude a su niño a aprender más sobre la playa escogiendo alguna de las actividades a continuación.

LIBROS ACERCA DE LA PLAYA:

Ayude a su niño a aprender más sobre la playa visitando la biblioteca. Busque libros como *El duende del mar* por Hilda Perera, *El pescador* por Fiona Moodie y *El amigo que vino del mar* por Mariano Vara.

EL CINE, LA MÚSICA Y MÁS:

Vean películas que transcurren en la playa o cerca de ella como *Treasure Island*, *Little Mermaid* o *Muppets Treasure Island*. Conversen sobre las playas que hayan visitado o visto. Busque cantos o rimas sobre la playa o el agua para cantar con su niño.

PROYECTO DE ARTE: Estrellas de mar

Materiales: papel de arte de color, cereal en formas redondeadas, tijeras, pegamento

Explíquele a su niño que las estrellas de mar viven en el mar y que tienen forma de estrella. Ayude a recortar la forma de una estrella en papel de color. Después pídale a su niño que pegue el cereal a la forma de estrella para crear una estrella de mar.

PARA COMPARTIR:

Ayude a su niño a crear criaturas de playa para la bañera. Pídale que recuerde las criaturas de la playa sobre las cuáles aprendió en el libro *Criaturas de la playa*. Proporciónele esponjas de color, marcadores y tijeras para así crear alguna de las criaturas de mar.

INTRODUCING *EN PAREJAS*

Introduce the subject of careers. Display the two books. Tell children that one of these books is about having many career choices when you grow up, and the other book shows what it is like to choose a career as an astronaut. *(Uno de los libros es sobre las alternativas de profesiones que pueden tener para escoger cuando crezcan. El otro libro es sobre la profesión de astronauta.)* Have children tell what kind of jobs they think they would like when they grow up. *(¿Qué tipo de trabajo quieren tener cuando sean grande?)* Invite the children to brainstorm what they know about careers. *(Díganme qué saben de las profesiones, de los trabajos que hacen las personas y de cómo aprenden las personas a hacer esos trabajos.)*

Podré ser lo que quiera

Two children think about the careers they might have when they grow up: vet, singer, astronaut, and more. In the end they are content to enjoy being kids.

Key Words:
veterinario
pianista
maestro
astronauta
dentista
acróbata
piloto
cantante

Objetives:
Reading Strategy: Making inferences
Language Pattern: Identifying naming words
Phonics Focus: Identifying the medial /r/ sound between vowels

¡Despegue!

This photo essay shows what astronauts do in space. The text tells about a variety of famous astronauts and their accomplishments.

Key Words:
norteamericano
canadiense
los Estados Unidos
especiales
el espacio

Objetives:
Reading Strategy: Making generalizations
Language Pattern: Identifying describing words
Phonics Focus: Reviewing *r* blends

Additional Components:
Audio Cassette Tape: *Podré ser lo que quiera*
¡Despegue!
Writing Masters, pages 73–77

Other Books About Careers
El teatro de sombras, Michael Ende
Diego, Jeanette and Jonah Winter

49

Podré ser lo que quiera

BEFORE READING

Ask children what they would like to be when they grow up. (*¿Qué quieren ser cuando crezcan?*) List their choices. Show the book cover and read aloud the title. Ask children what they think the title is referring to. (*¿A qué creen que se refiere el título?*) Have children make predictions about the book.

READING

Set a purpose for reading. Ask children to consider what the boy and girl are doing in the pictures. (*¿Qué están haciendo el niño y la niña en las ilustraciones?*) Have them describe what kinds of jobs the children are doing and the responsibilities that might be involved. (*Díganme qué tipos de trabajos están haciendo y qué responsabilidades tiene cada uno.*)

Use questions such as these to guide the reading:
- *¿Cuáles de los trabajos que se mencionan aquí les gustaría hacer cuando crezcan?*
- *¿Qué cosas creen que pueden aprender ahora que les ayudaría a hacer ese trabajo luego?*
- *¿Qué tipo de cosas necesita aprender a hacer la persona que hace ese trabajo?*

AFTER READING

Talk about the things the children did in this book. (*Hablemos de lo que los niños hicieron en el cuento.*) Review the pre-reading predictions. Ask children if they would be interested in any of the careers in this story. (*¿Les interesa alguna de las profesiones en el cuento?*) Add new ideas to the list of things children can be when they grow up. Challenge children to think of jobs they can do while they are still young.

Response Activities

Podré ser …
Materials: drawing paper, markers, crayons, pencils

Ask children to review the list of possible careers you've recorded so far and choose a career they would like to try. (*Repasen la lista de profesiones y escojan una que les gustaría probar.*) Have children illustrate themselves on the job and write what they would do at work. (*Dibújense en el trabajo y escriban lo que hacen.*)

Job Collage
Materials: old magazines, scissors, glue, large butcher paper, pencils

Have children work in small groups, searching for photos of people doing different jobs. Have each small group add pictures to a class collage.

MINI LESSONS

• READING STRATEGY
Making Inferences

Using self-stick notes, cover the job titles on each page and reread the book. Ask children to help you fill in the missing words. Tell them to use the illustrations as clues to make guesses about the words. (*Díganme las palabras que faltan. Usen las ilustraciones como claves para adivinar las palabras.*) Record their ideas on the self-stick notes. Then compare them to the actual text.

• LANGUAGE PATTERN
Identifying Naming Words

Have children identify the careers mentioned in the story as you write each career name on an index card (*pintor, veterinario, dentista, pianista, cantante, campeón de carreras de auto, campeón de tenis, acróbata, bailarín, maestro, escritor, piloto, astronauta*). Then have a volunteer find one of the career names in the book and match it to its card. Continue in this manner until all of the cards have been identified.

PHONICS FOCUS

Identifying the Medial /r/ Sound Between Vowels

Explain that the medial /r/ sound between vowels is represented by the letter *r*. Reread the story, asking children to make the /r/ sound every time they identify that sound between vowels. (*Hagan el sonido /r/ cada vez que lo oigan en medio de vocales: queramos, pintora, pintaré.*) When you are finished reading, write the words on the board, asking volunteers to read them aloud and circle the letter *r* in the medial position.

¡Despegue!

BEFORE READING

Read aloud the book title and ask children to explain the meaning of *¡Despegue!* and where they may have heard it. *(Explíquenme lo que quiere decir la palabra ¡Despegue! y dónde la han escuchado.)* Allow several possible definitions. Then show the cover photo and ask children to predict what the book might be about. *(¿Sobre qué creen que trata este libro?)*

READING

Set a purpose for reading. Ask children to define the word *astronauta*. Have them point to all of the astronauts in the book. *(Muéstrenme todos los astronautas en el libro.)* Ask children to talk about what the astronauts are doing in each picture. *(Díganme qué están haciendo los astronautas en cada ilustración.)*

Use questions such as these to guide the reading:
- ¿Por qué van los astronautas al espacio?
- ¿Quién puede ser un astronauta?
- ¿Cómo se mueven los astronautas en el espacio?

AFTER READING

Talk about the pictures and the information in *¡Despegue!* Have children share what they have learned about astronauts and space. *(Compartan lo que han aprendido sobre los astronautas y sobre el espacio.)* Review the children's predictions about the book. Then ask children to recall the names of some of the astronauts in the book. *(Díganme los nombres de algunos de los astronautas en el libro.)*

Response Activities

Space Log
Materials: paper, pencils, crayons

Ask children to imagine that they are on the moon and need to record their observations in a space log. *(Imagínense que están en la Luna y necesitan anotar sus observaciones.)* Encourage children to write about and illustrate their voyage, their feelings, and what they have seen and discovered.

Voy a la Luna
Materials: none

With the whole class, play this variation of "I'm Going on a Picnic." The first person says, *Voy a la Luna y voy a llevar _____.* They fill in the blank with what they will take along to the moon. The second person repeats what the first person said and adds a new item, and so on.

MINI LESSONS

• READING STRATEGY
Making Generalizations

Tell children, *Una generalización es una declaración que generalmente o usualmente es cierta.* Invite children to make generalizations about astronauts, based on the information and photos in the book. Lead them to draw such conclusions as the following: *Los astronautas tienen que estar en buena condición física. Los astronautas trabajan muy duro. Los astronautas deben ser muy valientes para volar en el espacio.*

• LANGUAGE PATTERN
Identifying Describing Words

Reread the text with children. Say, *Fíjense en las palabras* norteamericano *y* canadiense. *Estas palabras describen de dónde vienen los astronautas.* Write on the board *trajes especiales* and *la bandera de los Estados Unidos.* For each phrase have children identify the words that give details about something. Then ask children to find other words in the book that describe details about objects.

PHONICS FOCUS

Reviewing *r* Blends

Ask children to listen carefully so they can identify all the *r* blends in the story. *(Presten atención para que puedan identificar las palabras que tengan combinaciones con la letra* r.*)* Reread the story, asking children to roll their *r*'s every time they hear a word with an *r* blend. As they do, write that word on the board (ast*r*onautas, t*r*abajan, ent*r*enan, ap*r*ender, p*r*actican, t*r*ajes, p*r*imer, p*r*imera). When you are finished reading, ask volunteers to go to the board, read a word, and circle the *r* blend.

51

Tying the Pair Together

Display the two books. Ask, *¿En qué son los libros semejantes or diferentes? ¿Cuál es ficción y cuál es no-ficción?* Have children tell what they have learned about careers, including being an astronaut. *(¿Qué han aprendido sobre las profesiones incluyendo el ser astronauta?)* Ask them to share what they now know about different kinds of jobs. *(Compartan lo que saben sobre los diferentes trabajos y cómo la gente aprende a hacer estos trabajos.)*

Creative Dramatics: Pantomime
Materials: none

Ask a volunteer to pantomime a job they would like to do when they grow up. *(Hagan una pantomima sobre las profesiones que quisieran hacer cuando sean grandes.)* Tell others to try to guess the career. Have children take turns performing a pantomime until several different careers have been demonstrated.

Social Studies: Whom Do You Help?
Materials: none

Create a list of jobs, using any new ideas from the children, and ask them to identify who these people help. *(¿A quiénes ayudan estas personas?)* For example, *¿A quién ayuda un doctor? ¿A quién ayuda el presidente? ¿A quién ayuda el astronauta?* Make a chart to record each of these questions and their answers.

Social Studies/Gathering Information: Jobs at School
Materials: paper, pencils

Have children list the jobs people do at their school. Help children decide on four or five questions to ask about each job. *(Hagan una lista de los trabjajos que hace la gente en la escuela. Decidan sobre cuatro o cinco preguntas para hacerles acerca de sus trabajos.)* Ask some of these workers to come talk to your class so the children can interview them.

ASSESSMENT

- Ask children to tell what they have learned about careers and space. *(¿Qué han aprendido sobre las profesiones y sobre el espacio?)* Record and date these responses.
- Review the objectives given in the lessons for *Podré ser lo que quiera* and *¡Despegue!* Place samples of children's work on these objectives in their portfolios.
- Use informal conferencing with children to assess reading, language, and phonics skills they have learned from the books.

For further assessment ideas and checklists, see pages 78–80.

Home Activities

Copy and distribute to children the *Llévame a casa* activity master found on page 54. At home children can look through the newspaper for space-related news.

Tie It to English

LISTENING/SPEAKING/WRITING

Identifying Professions
Vocabulary Words/Phrases: *mail carrier, police officer, doctor, schoolteacher*

Explain to children that in addition to the jobs mentioned in the book, there are other jobs such as mail carrier, police officer, doctor, and schoolteacher. Write these jobs on the board and have pairs of children choose one of the occupations. One partner should make a drawing representative of the job, and the other partner should write the name of the job below the drawing.

VIEWING/WRITING

Distribute copies of the activity below. Have children draw a line to match each person to his or her work place. Encourage children to choose a job name from the box below and write it in the appropriate space.

| mail carrier | doctor | police officer | schoolteacher |

53

LLÉVAME A CASA

Estimada familia de _____,

ACTIVIDADES SOBRE LAS PROFESIONES

Su niño ha leído sobre diferentes trabajos o profesiones que tal vez pudiera hacer algún día. El libro *Podré ser lo que quiera* trata de dos niños que piensan en los varios trabajos que pueden hacer cuando crezcan, incluyendo ser astronautas. *¡Despegue!* muestra lo que hacen los astronautas en el espacio y habla de los acontecimientos logrados por varios astronautas famosos. Ayude a su niño a aprender más sobre ser astronautas y otras profesiones escogiendo alguna de las actividades a continuación.

LIBROS ACERCA DE LAS PROFESIONES:

Ayude a su niño a aprender más sobre las profesiones visitando la biblioteca. Busque libros como *El teatro de sombras* por Michael Ende y *Diego* por Jeanette y Jonah Winter.

PROYECTOS DE ARTE: Tarjetas de presentación

Materiales: tarjetas de índice, creyones o marcadores

Creen tarjetas de presentación para su familia y sus amistades. Haga que su niño decida el título de cada persona. Anímelo a recordar las profesiones en *Podré ser lo que quiera*. Déle las tarjetas y los marcadores a su niño y ayúdelo a escribir el nombre, título, dirección y número de teléfono de cada persona. Invite a su niño a usar las tarjetas de presentación para asignar un lugar para sentarse en la mesa a cada miembro de la familia.

EL CINE, LA MÚSICA Y MÁS:

Vean películas sobre viajes espaciales, como *Apollo 13* o biografías de personas famosas. Ayude a su niño a investigar la carrera que le interese para aprender más sobre ella.

Busque cantos o rimas sobre trabajos o carreras para cantar con su niño.

PARA COMPARTIR:

Haga los arreglos necesarios para que su niño pueda visitarlo a usted o a un miembro de su familia en el trabajo. Ayúdelo a pensar en preguntas que hacer como cuáles son las responsabilidades o el horario de cierto trabajo.

54

INTRODUCING *EN PAREJAS*

Invite children to describe what they know about their school. *(Descríbanme qué saben de su escuela.)* List their ideas on the board or on chart paper. Ask them to name types of things they enjoy at school. *(Díganme cuáles son las actividades que disfrutan en la escuela.)* Display the two books, and encourage children to tell what they know about them from the titles and pictures on the book covers. *(¿Qué pueden decir de estos libros al mirar las ilustraciones y las portadas?)*

El paseo escolar de Luis

On the day of the class field trip to the zoo, Luis has difficulty keeping track of his lunch box. In the end, Luis enjoys lunch at the zoo after all.

Key Words:
el mono
el elefante
la cebra
la jirafa

Objectives:
Reading Strategy: Summarizing the story
Language Pattern: Identifying naming words
Phonics Focus: Identifying the digraphs *ch* and *ll*

Escuelas de todo el mundo

This photo essay provides children opportunities to compare and contrast their own school experiences with those of school children around the world.

Key Words:
caminamos
visitamos
usamos
escribimos
aprendemos
practicamos

Objectives:
Reading Strategy: Comparing and contrasting experiences
Language Pattern: Identifying action words
Phonics Focus: Identifying diphthongs

Additional Components:

Audio Cassette Tape: *El paseo escolar de Luis*
Escuelas de todo el mundo
Writing Masters, pages 73–77

Other Books About Schools

Me gustan los libros, Liliana Santirso
Timoteo va a la escuela, Rosemary Wells

El paseo escolar de Luis

BEFORE READING

Ask children to tell about a school trip they have taken. What was it like? Did they lose anything? *(Cuéntenme sobre algún paseo escolar al que hayan ido. ¿Cómo fue el paseo? ¿Se les perdió algo?)* Show the cover of the book, read the title, and ask children to predict what they think will happen. *(Miren la cubierta del libro, lean el título y díganme sobre qué creen que tratará el libro.)*

READING

Set a purpose for reading by asking children to think about where Luis' class might be going. *(¿Adónde creen que va la clase de Luis?)* Encourage them to connect happenings in the book to occurrences in their everyday lives.

Use questions such as these to guide the reading:
- ¿Cómo se siente uno cuando está tan alegre que no puede pensar?
- ¿Qué creen que piensan el papá, la maestra y el chofer del autobús cuando le entregan la lonchera a Luis?
- ¿Por qué pensó Luis que el elefante, la cebra y la jirafa se estaban comiendo su almuerzo?

AFTER READING

Ask children how they think Luis felt when he found his lunch and backpack. *(¿Cómo creen que se sintió Luis cuando encontró su mochila y su almuerzo?)* Invite children to brainstorm other ways Luis could have kept track of his lunch box. *(Quiero que piensen en algunas formas en que Luis hubiera podido seguirle el rastro a su lonchera.)*

Response Activities

Too Happy to Think!
Materials: drawing paper, markers

Remind children how the book began with the sentence, *¡Luis estaba tan alegre que no podía pensar!* Invite children to draw a picture of something they think Luis was happy about *(a particular animal, riding a bus, being with his friends, etc.). (Dibujen algo por lo que Luis pudiera estar alegre [un animal en particular, pasear en autobús, estar con sus amigos, etc.].* Then have children share their pictures. On the board make a list of their ideas about why Luis was so happy.

MINI LESSONS

• READING STRATEGY
Summarizing the Story

Ask children to tell about the story in one to three sentences: *La clase de Luis fue al zoológico. Luis perdió su almuerzo. Luis almorzó con todos.* Help children see how the sentences sum up the ideas of the story.

• LANGUAGE PATTERN
Identifying Naming Words

Have children recall words from the story that name animals: *los monos, los elefantes, las cebras, las jirafas.* Help children locate these words in the book. Ask them to describe strategies they used to locate each word. *(Díganme las estrategias que utilizaron para localizar cada palabra.)*

PHONICS FOCUS

Identifying the Digraphs *ch* and *ll*

Explain to children that double l (*ll*) and c, h (*ch*) are two letter combinations that represent a sound different from that of the original letters. *(La doble l (ll) y la c, h (ch) son dos combinaciones de letras que representan un sonido diferente al de las letras originales.)* Write examples on the board *(llorar, chaqueta)*. Reread the story, asking children to clap once when they hear the *ll* combination and twice when they hear the *ch* combination. *(Den una palmada cada vez que oigan el sonido de la combinación de la doble l (ll) y dos palmadas cuando oigan el sonido de la combinación c y h (ch).)*

¡OJO! Although the word *lonchera* is borrowed from the English, it has become so popular and widely used that it is better known than the word *fiambrera*.

Escuelas de todo el mundo

BEFORE READING

Invite children to tell what they know about schools in other countries. *(Cuenten lo que saben sobre las escuelas en otros países.)* Create a chart with the headings What We Know *(Lo que sabemos)* and What We Want to Know *(Lo que queremos saber)*. Then introduce the book. Ask children to look at the cover photograph to predict what they think they will learn about other schools. *(Miren la portada y díganme qué creen que aprenderán sobre otras escuelas.)*

READING

Tell children they will be reading a book in which the photographs provide much information about the setting and the life of school children all over the world. *(Van a leer un libro en el cual las fotografías les darán mucha información sobre el ambiente y la vida escolar de niños de todo el mundo.)* Guide them to compare these schools to their own experiences as they read.

Use questions such as these to guide the reading:
- ¿En qué se parecen tu escuela y las escuelas de los niños en el libro? ¿En qué son diferentes?
- ¿Cómo van ustedes a la escuela?
- ¿Cómo pasan el día en la escuela?

AFTER READING

Encourage children to tell what they learned about schools around the world. *(¿Qué han aprendido sobre las escuelas de todo el mundo?)* List their ideas on the chart paper from the Before Reading activity. Invite them to compare what they thought the book would be about to the list of what they learned. *(Comparen lo que ustedes pensaron que este libro iba a tratar con la lista de lo que aprendieron.)*

Response Activities

Where Is It?
Materials: world map

Locate the countries in *Escuelas de todo el mundo* on the world map. Invite groups of children to locate the country closest to the United States and also the country farthest away from the United States. *(Busquen el país que está más cerca de los Estados Unidos y también el país que está más lejos de los Estados Unidos.)*

MINI LESSONS

- **READING STRATEGY**

Comparing and Contrasting Experiences

Ask children what they learned from reading *Escuelas de todo el mundo*. *(¿Qué han aprendido de este libro?)* Have them tell how their own school experiences are similar or different. *(Díganme en qué las experiencias escolares son semejantes o diferentes a las de ustedes.)* Help children make some generalizations about how they are like children around the world.

- **LANGUAGE PATTERN**

Identifying Action Words

Write *caminamos* and *escribimos* on the board. Tell children that these words show a specific action. *(Estas palabras denotan una acción específica.)* Have children find other action words in the book. *(Busquen otras palabras de acción en el libro.)* Then ask volunteers to select one of these action words to pantomime as others try to guess the word.

PHONICS FOCUS

Identifying Diphthongs

Review with children that a diphthong is a combination of two vowels pronounced as one sound. *(Un diptongo es una combinación de dos vocales pronunciadas como un sólo sonido: j<u>ue</u>go, pat<u>io</u>.)* As you reread the story, ask children to say the word ¡diptongo! every time they hear one. Write the following words on the board and call on volunteers to underline the letters forming each diphthong: esc<u>ue</u>la, n<u>ue</u>stra, <u>ai</u>re.

Tying the Pair Together

Display the two books and encourage children to compare and contrast them. Ask children how they are the same and different. *(Quiero que comparen estos dos libros. Díganme en qué son parecidos y en qué son diferentes.)* Have children share what they have learned about schools and field trips. *(Compartan lo que han aprendido sobre las escuelas y los paseos escolares.)*

Nutrition: What's for Lunch?
Materials: writing paper, pencils

Invite children to list foods they might take to school in a lunch box. *(Hagan una lista de los alimentos que ustedes llevarían a la escuela en una lonchera.)* Have them discuss the pictures in *El paseo escolar de Luis* and *Escuelas de todo el mundo* and talk about what other foods children might take to school. *(¿Qué alimentos creen que llevarían otros niños a la escuela?)* Lead them to understand that children around the world sometimes eat different kinds of food.

Science: What's the Weather?
Materials: copies of *El paseo escolar de Luis* and *Escuelas de todo el mundo*, paper

Encourage children to study the illustrations and photographs in both books to determine if the climate is hot or cold in each picture. *(Observen bien las ilustraciones y las fotografías en ambos libros para determinar si el clima es caliente o frío.)* Compare the climates in the different countries to the climate where Luis lives. *(Comparen el clima en los diferentes países con el clima donde vive Luis.)* Have children write a sentence about where they live and how it compares to one of the places in the photographs. *(Escriban una oración acerca del lugar donde viven y cómo se compara a una de estas fotografías.)*

Geography: Animals Around the World
Materials: books about animals, globe

Write the names of the countries from *Escuelas de todo el mundo* on the board. Together with children review the location of these countries on the world map or globe. Then ask children where they think the animals in *El paseo escolar de Luis* came from. *(¿De dónde creen que son los animales que aparecen en* El paseo escolar de Luis*?)* Use books about animals to discuss which animals might have come from which countries.

ASSESSMENT

- Ask children to tell what they have learned about different schools. Record and date these responses. *(¿Qué han aprendido sobre las diferentes escuelas?)*
- Review the objectives given in the lessons for *El paseo escolar de Luis* and *Escuelas de todo el mundo*. Place samples of children's work on the objectives in their portfolios.
- Use informal conferencing with children to assess reading, language, and phonics skills they have learned from the books.

Home Activities

Copy and distribute to children the *Llévame a casa* activity master found on page 60. Tell children to ask their families to describe the schools they attended in first grade. *(Pídanles a sus familias que describan las escuelas a las que ellos asistieron en primer grado.)*

Tie It to English

LISTENING/SPEAKING/READING

Identifying Action Words
Vocabulary Words: *walk, wear, learn, visit, write*

Write the vocabulary words on the board. Model pronunciation of each word as you explain its meaning to children. Point out that the word *visit* is very similar to *visitar* in Spanish. Ask children to open their copy of *Escuelas de todo el mundo*. Ask volunteers on what page they think they can find the Spanish word for *walk* (*caminamos*, p. 2). Continue with other vocabulary words, asking children to find the corresponding Spanish words on pages 3, 9, 10, and 12. Have each child say a simple sentence using one of the vocabulary words.

READING/VIEWING/WRITING

Reviewing Action Words

Distribute copies of the activity below. Have children complete each sentence by writing the letter for the appropriate word on the line.

---

1. We walk _____ .   a.

2. We wear _____ .   b.

3. We learn _____ .   c.

4. We write _____ .   d.

59

LLÉVAME A CASA

Estimada familia de _____,

ACTIVIDADES SOBRE LAS ESCUELAS

Su niño ha leído sobre las experiencias nuevas que tienen los niños en sus escuelas y en los paseos escolares. *El paseo escolar de Luis* cuenta como Luis no puede recordar adónde dejó su lonchera. El otro libro, *Escuelas de todo el mundo*, es un ensayo fotográfico de escuelas en diferentes lugares. Ayude a su niño a aprender más sobre los paseos escolares y las escuelas realizando algunas de las actividades siguientes.

LIBROS ACERCA DE LAS ESCUELAS:

Ayude a su niño a aprender más sobre las diferentes clases de escuelas. Visiten juntos la biblioteca local y busquen libros como *Me gustan los libros* por Liliana Santirso y *Timoteo va a la escuela* por Rosemary Wells.

EL CINE, LA MÚSICA Y MÁS:

Busque los videos de *El autobús mágico* y lleve a su niño a pasear con la clase de la señorita Frizzle. Juntos pueden escoger cuál de los diferentes lugares quieren ir a visitar. Conversen acerca de las diferencias entre estos destinos fantásticos a los paseos reales que su niño haya hecho con su escuela.

Busque cantos o rimas tradicionales sobre la escuela para cantar con su niño.

PROYECTO DE ARTE: Creando loncheras

Materiales: caja pequeña de cartón cubierta con papel de arte blanco, etiquetas engomadas, marcadores, papel de envolver, papel de arte, pegamento

Con su niño, haga una lonchera como la que tiene Luis en *El paseo escolar de Luis*. Pídale a su niño que recuerde cómo era la lonchera y qué tenía adentro. Una vez construida la lonchera, pídale a su niño que la decore cómo quiera.

PARA COMPARTIR:

Ayude a su niño a hacer una lista de las actividades que hace en la escuela. Pídale que recuerde lo que hacían los niños en la escuela en *Escuelas de todo el mundo*.

INTRODUCING *EN PAREJAS*

Display a photograph of a dinosaur skeleton and ask children to guess what animal they think it belongs to. *(¿De qué animal creen que es este esqueleto?)* Show children pictures of fossils and have them try to name the animals. Ask them whether they think there are any dinosaurs alive today. *(¿Creen que existen dinosaurios hoy en día?)* Invite them to share any facts they may know about dinosaurs. *(Díganme qué saben de los dinosaurios.)* List, date, and initial children's responses.

Muestra y cuenta entre dinosaurios

Daniel the dinosaur can't think of anything to share for *Muestra y cuenta*. Then he amazes his prehistoric classmates by bringing in something they've never seen before—a human!

Key Words:
algo
llevar
se dijo
compartir
la hora de la lectura
piedras

Objectives:
Reading Strategy: Identifying categories
Language Pattern: Identifying repetitive dialogue
Phonics Focus: Reviewing the /y/ sound

¿Cómo eran los dinosaurios?

Interesting facts about dinosaurs are related to objects children will recognize in this photo essay on dinosaurs' size, weight, and eating habits.

Key Words:
braquiosaurio
heterodontosaurio
esteagosaurio
triceratops

Objectives:
Reading Strategy: Recognizing comparisons
Language Pattern: Identifying naming words
Phonics Focus: Reviewing the /l/ sound in the initial and medial positions

Additional Components:
Audio Cassette Tape: *Muestra y cuenta entre dinosaurios*
¿Cómo eran los dinosaurios?
Writing Masters, pages 73–77

Other Books About Dinosaurs
Danielito y el dinosaurio, Syd Hoff
Destello el dinosaurio, Marcus Pfister
Alex quiere un dinosaurio, Hiawyn Oram and Satoshi Kitamura

Muestra y cuenta entre dinosaurios

BEFORE READING

Show children a collection of items, such as rocks or shells. Invite them to tell about items they might bring for Show and Tell. *(Cuéntenme sobre los artículos que quieran traer a clase para Muestra y cuenta—una colección, un juguete especial o una mascota.)* Display the book. Ask children to use the cover illustration and title to guess what the dinosaurs in this story will bring.

READING

Set a purpose for reading by pointing out that some things the characters choose to bring are collections and some are special for other reasons. *(Algunas de las cosas que traen los personajes son colecciones y otras son especiales por otras razones.)* As they read, help children think about the categories in which these items belong.

Use questions such as these to guide the reading:
- ¿En qué es diferente la colección de insectos de Diana a colecciones de insectos verdaderas?
- ¿Dónde mantiene Toni su colección?
- ¿Cómo se siente Daniel antes de saber lo que va a llevar?

AFTER READING

✴ Talk about the collections, favorite things, and pets in the story. Ask children if the items the characters share remind them of something they own. *(¿Les recuerdan los artículos de los personajes algo que ustedes tienen?)* Discuss the children's Before Reading predictions and have them consider whether or not their predictions match what the author wrote.

Response Activities

Dinosaur Dialogue
Materials: none

Explain to children that this story is written in dialogue. *(Este cuento ha sido escrito en diálogo.)* Have them choose parts and read it aloud. Then divide the class into groups. Ask children to write things the characters might say after they see Paco. *(Escriban lo que podrían decir los personajes al ver a Paco.)* Then have them role-play these characters, using the dialogue they have written.

Prehistoric Classrooms
Materials: drawing paper, crayons

Discuss some of the prehistoric details in the illustrations, such as the stone tablets or the flat globe. Have children brainstorm names of other objects for a prehistoric classroom *(sillas hechas de piedras, cortinas hechas de hojas grandes)*. Have children draw their ideas and display their pictures.

MINI LESSONS

• READING STRATEGY
Identifying Categories

Explain to children the meaning of categories and provide examples. Ask children to imagine that they are each going to bring one item for *Muestra y cuenta* that would be in the category of nature. *(Cada uno de ustedes va a traer algo en la categoría de la naturaleza.)* Then have children think of a new category, such as things that are small *(cosas que son pequeñas)* or things that are blue *(cosas que son azules)*, and continue the activity.

• LANGUAGE PATTERN
Identifying Repetitive Dialogue

Open the book to page 4 and ask children if they can tell who is talking and what is being said. *(Lean la página 4 y díganme quién está hablando y qué están diciendo.)* Then ask children to turn to pages 6, 7, and 8 and tell you who the characters are talking with. *(Miren las páginas 6, 7 y 8 y díganme con quién están hablando los personajes.)* [Están hablándose a sí mismos, o pensando en voz alta.]

PHONICS FOCUS

Reviewing the /y/ Sound

Review with children the /y/ sound, which is represented by the letter combination *ll*. On the board write *ll*. Reread the story, asking children to repeat after you the words with the /y/ sound. *(Repitan las palabras que llevan el sonido /y/: llevar, llevaré, estampillas, llevó.)* Ask children to think of other words with the /y/ sound, such as *silla, calle, lluvia,* and *pollo*. Write them on the board and ask volunteers to underline the letter combination *ll*.

✴ **¡OJO!** In some Spanish-speaking countries, stamps are known as *sellos* as well as *estampillas*.

¿Cómo eran los dinosaurios?

BEFORE READING

Ask children to name any dinosaurs they know. *(Nombren cualquier dinosaurio que conozcan.)* List the names on chart paper and have children add any facts they know about that type of dinosaur. Use these facts to make a chart of What We Know *(Lo que sabemos)* and What We Want to Know *(Lo que queremos saber)*. Read the book title and ask children to predict what dinosaurs they think will be included.

READING

Set a purpose for reading by asking children to think about what kind of book this is. *(¿Qué tipo de libro creen que es éste?)* Refer to the chart from the previous activity and encourage children to look for additional facts as they read.

Use questions such as these to guide the reading:
- ¿Cuál es el dinosaurio más pequeño mencionado en el libro?
- ¿Comen los dinosaurios la misma comida? Expliquen.
- ¿Qué claves tenemos que de verdad alguna vez existieron los dinosaurios?

AFTER READING

Discuss the dinosaur facts in the book. Ask children to tell about any new facts they have learned and add them to the Before Reading chart. *(Díganme cualquier dato nuevo que aprendieron.)* Tell children to use the text and photos to find facts and tell about anything that surprised them. *(Usen el texto y las fotografías para buscar datos y hablar de cualquier cosa que les sorprendió.)*

Response Activities

Dinosaur Dig
Materials: dinosaur books, art paper, crayons, scissors

Using dinosaur books for reference, have children draw their favorite dinosaur, cut it out, and write their own name on the back. Collect the cutouts and ask children to cover their eyes as you hide the dinosaurs around the classroom. Then have children go on a dig to find and identify the dinosaurs.

Signs for a Dinosaur Park
Materials: markers, poster board

Ask children to imagine that they are time-traveling to visit a live dinosaur zoo. *(Imagínense que están viajando por el tiempo a visitar un zoológico de dinosaurios.)* Have children work together to write a list of rules people would need to follow. *(Escriban una lista de reglas que la gente debe seguir.)* Have children write their rules on poster board to create signs.

MINI LESSONS

• READING STRATEGY
Recognizing Comparisons

Ask children, ¿Qué tan grande es un dinosaurio? ¿Cómo les ayuda el libro a saberlo? Lead them to discuss how phrases like *tan alto como, tan pequeño como, tan largo como,* and *tan pesado como* help them compare dinosaur sizes to things that they know. Have them tell how the pictures provide information. *(Explíquenme cómo las fotos les dan información sobre el tamaño de los dinosaurios en comparación a las cosas que ustedes ya conocen.)*

• LANGUAGE PATTERN
Identifying Naming Words

Point out that most dinosaur names end with *-saurio*. Reread the story and invite children to chime in on the dinosaur names. Then print each name on a piece of construction paper and cut it out in the shape of a dinosaur footprint. Scatter the footprints around the room to form a trail. Help children "follow the dinosaur" by reading each word along the trail.

PHONICS FOCUS

Reviewing the /l/ Sound in the Initial and Medial Positions

Write the letter *l* on the board as you review with children that the /l/ sound is represented by this letter. Reread the story to the children, asking them to tap their desk when they hear the /l/ sound in the initial, or medial position. *(Den un golpe en sus pupitres cada vez que oigan el sonido /l/ en posición inicial o en el medio.)*

63

Tying the Pair Together

Display copies of *Muestra y cuenta entre dinosaurios* and *¿Cómo eran los dinosaurios?* Have children discuss similarities and differences between the two books. *(Díganme en qué son semejantes estos libros y en qué son diferentes.)* Lead them to conclude that while both books are about dinosaurs, one is real and the other is make-believe. Have them refer to the illustrations and photographs to compare the dinosaurs that appear in both books.

Writing: Dinosaur Names
Materials: art paper, crayons

Remind children that dinosaurs are frequently named for their body characteristics. (*Triceratops*, for example, means *three horns*.) *(Con frecuencia los dinosaurios reciben sus nombres por las características de sus cuerpos. Por ejemplo,* triceratops *significa* tres cuernos.) Using the word stem *-saurio*, invite children to make up a name for a new kind of dinosaur and draw a picture that conveys its name. *(Por ejemplo, un dinosuario con lunares podría llamarse "lunarsaurio".)*

Science: Learning About Skeletons
Materials: pictures of human or dinosaur skeletons, toothpicks, glue, art paper

Explain that people have learned a lot about dinosaurs from studying their skeletons. *(Hemos aprendido mucho sobre los dinosaurios estudiando sus esqueletos.)* Show children a picture or a model of a human skeleton. Then show a photograph of a dinosaur skeleton. *(Díganme las diferencias y las semejanzas entre las cabezas, las patas, los brazos y los cuerpos de los dinosaurios y de los humanos.)* Then have children make any type of skeleton from toothpicks and glue it to art paper.

Creative Arts: Dinosaur Models
Materials: modeling clay

Suggest that children use the illustrations and photographs from this theme as a guide for creating their own clay dinosaur models. Let models dry overnight. After their models have dried, children can group them according to size and create a dinosaur exhibit for another class to visit.

ASSESSMENT

- Ask children to tell what they have learned about dinosaurs. *(Díganme qué han aprendido sobre los dinosaurios.)* Record and date these responses.
- Review the objectives given in the lessons for *Muestra y cuenta entre dinosaurios* and *¿Cómo eran los dinosaurios?* Place samples of children's work on these objectives in their portfolios.
- Use informal conferencing with children to assess reading, language, and phonics skills they have learned from the books.

For further assessment ideas and checklists, see pages 78–80.

Home Activities

Copy and distribute to children the *Llévame a casa* activity master found on page 66. Tell children to share with family members dinosaur information. *(Compartan con sus familias información sobre los dinosaurios.)*

Tie It to English

LISTENING/SPEAKING/VIEWING

Expressing Comparisons
Vocabulary Words/Phrases: *big (bigger than); small (smaller than); tall (taller than); heavy (heavier than)*

Display pictures of a skyscraper, an ant, a giraffe, and an elephant. Use the pictures to introduce the vocabulary words and phrases. Then go through the book *¿Cómo eran los dinosaurios?*, reinforcing the meaning of each word. Ask children, *Is a dinosaur bigger than you? Is an ant bigger than a dinosaur?* Have children draw animals of different sizes and then compare them. Ask, *Is (María's) dinosaur taller than (Juan's) dog? Whose animal is heavier than this tiger?*

READING/WRITING/SPEAKING

Distribute copies of the activity below. Have children read each sentence, choose an appropriate phrase from the box below, and write it in the space provided. When children are finished, call on them to read their choices to the class.

---

bigger than   smaller than   taller than

1. The giraffe is _____ _____ the man.

2. The dog is _____ _____ the car.

3. The dinosaur is _____ _____ the mouse.

LLÉVAME A CASA

Estimada familia de _____,

ACTIVIDADES SOBRE LOS DINOSAURIOS

Aprender sobre los dinosaurios es algo que le gusta a la mayoría de los niños. Su niño ha estado aprendiendo y leyendo sobre este tema. *Muestra y cuenta entre dinosaurios* es acerca de un dinosaurio que no sabe qué traer a clase para mostrar y contar. *¿Cómo eran los dinosaurios?* es sobre el tamaño, el peso y los hábitos de comida de las diferentes clases de dinosaurios. Ayude a su niño a aprender más sobre los dinosaurios escogiendo algunas de las actividades a continuación.

LIBROS ACERCA DE LOS DINOSAURIOS:

Ayude a su niño a aprender más sobre los dinosaurios visitando la bibilioteca. Busque libros como *Danielito y el dinosaurio* por Syd Hoff, *Destello el dinosaurio* por Marcus Pfister y *Alex quiere un dinosaurio* por Hiawyn Oram y Satoshi Kitamura.

EL CINE, LA MÚSICA Y MÁS:

Vean películas sobre los dinosaurios como *The Land Before Time*. Pídale a su niño que identifique los dinosaurios que reconoce en la película. Busque o invente canciones sobre los dinosaurios para cantar con su niño.

PROYECTO DE ARTE: Dinosaurios de la calle

Materiales: tiza para escribir en la calle

Anime a su niño a pensar sobre diferentes dinosaurios. Ayúdelo a escoger y dibujar un dinosaurio grande afuera de su casa usando tiza de colores.

PARA COMPARTIR:

Ayude a su niño a hacer una lista de comidas que podrían comer los dinosaurios. Separe las listas entre los dinosaurios que comen carne (como un tiranosaurio) y los que comen plantas (como un braquiosaurio). Pídale a su niño que recuerde los datos que aprendió sobre los hábitos de comida de los dinosaurios. Pídale a su niño que seleccione alimentos del refrigerador y los separe en grupos de comida para los tiranosaurios y para los braquiosaurios.

INTRODUCING *EN PAREJAS*

Ask children what they know about wolves and record their ideas. *(¿Qué saben sobre los lobos?)* Then display the two books in the set, pointing out the wolves on the covers. Ask children how the wolves are the same and different. *(¿En qué son semejantes? ¿En qué son diferentes?)* If they haven't already mentioned stories in which there is a wolf character, ask them to tell about wolf stories they have read. *(Cuéntenme sobre libros o cuentos que conozcan donde uno de los personajes es un lobo.)*

Caperucita Roja y Lobo Feroz

Caperucita Roja uses her ingenuity to change Lobo Feroz' crafty ways. He then ends up joining Caperucita Roja and Abuelita for a tasty dinner.

Key Words:

preguntó   contestó
se dijo   llamó
gran   visitar
lamió   los labios

Objectives:
Reading Strategy: Predicting outcomes
Language Pattern: Demonstrating use of dialogue
Phonics Focus: Reviewing the /r/ sound

Los lobos

The variety of wolves shown and the areas in which they live make this informational photo book beautiful and interesting.

Key Words:

los lobos   el lobo
salvaje   invierno
cálidos

Objectives:
Reading Strategy: Categorizing information
Language Pattern: Identifying plural words
Phonics Focus: Reviewing the /b/ sound

Additional Components:

Big Books: *Caperucita Roja y Lobo Feroz*
             Los lobos
Audio Cassette Tape: *Caperucita Roja y Lobo Feroz*
             Los lobos
Writing Masters, pages 73–77

Other Books About Wolves

La verdadera historia de los tres cerditos, Jon Scieszka
Diez cuentos de lobos, Jean Francois Blade

Caperucita Roja y Lobo Feroz

BEFORE READING

Share the song *¿Quién le teme al lobo feroz?* ("Who's Afraid of the Big Bad Wolf?") with children, and invite them to sing along. Read aloud a traditional version of "Caperucita Roja." Ask children to predict what they think will happen in the book. *(¿Qué piensan que ocurrirá en el cuento?)* Help children use the cover illustration and the title to guess whether this book will be like or unlike the familiar story of "Caperucita Roja."

READING

Set a purpose for reading by discussing how pictures help tell a story. Take a picture walk through the book, stopping at page 12, not revealing the ending. Have children predict how it might end. *(Díganme cómo piensan que terminará este cuento.)* Then read the story together.

Use questions such as these to guide the reading:
- ¿Por qué Caperucita Roja iba a visitar a su abuelilta?
- ¿Con quién se encontró en el camino?
- ¿Por qué piensan que Caperuicta Roja sabía que Lobo Feroz la estaba siguiendo?

AFTER READING

Talk about this version of "Caperucita Roja." Discuss how the pictures help tell the story. *(Fíjense como las ilustraciones ayudan a contar el cuento.)* Ask children to describe what they think the pictures reveal about each character. *(¿Qué les dicen las ilustraciones sobre cada personaje?)*

Response Activities

Where Do We Go From Here?
Materials: board, chalk

On the way to Abuelita's house, Caperucita Roja made several stops. With children list information in categories on the board: *Dónde se detuvo, Con quién se encontró,* and *Qué le dieron.*

To Abuelita's House
Materials: art paper, crayons, small object to use as the figure

Have pairs of children draw maps of the path Caperucita Roja took to Abuelita's house. *(Dibujen un mapa del camino que tomó Caperucita Roja a casa de su abuelita.)* When children are finished, tell one child to give directions while the other child moves a small figure along the path, following the directions he or she is given.

MINI LESSONS

• READING STRATEGY
Predicting Outcomes

Have children retell the outcome in this version of "Caperucita Roja." Ask whether their Before Reading prediction was the same or different as the actual outcome. Have them share clues that helped them think about what might happen. *(¿Cuándo supieron que el lobo iba a ser amable? ¿Cómo hubiera sido diferente el cuento si la comida en la cesta no hubiera sido apetitosa para el lobo?)*

• LANGUAGE PATTERN
Demonstrating Use of Dialogue

Point out the use of quotation marks in the story. Tell children that these marks tell when a character is talking. *(Los signos ortográficos nos indican que el personaje está hablando.)* Also point to the words that indicate a character is about to speak or think: *preguntó, contestó, llamó, se dijo.* Assign character roles to children and have them read aloud parts of the story. Remind them to read with the expressions they think the characters used to say these lines. *(Lean con la emoción que creen que los personajes tenían cuando dijeron estas líneas.)*

PHONICS FOCUS

Reviewing the /r/ Sound

Review with children the /r/ sound, which is represented by the letter *r*. *(El sonido /r/ está representado por la letra r.)* Reread the story, asking children to clap when they hear the /r/ sound. *(Den una palmada cada vez que oigan el sonido /r/.)* Write the words on the board. Ask volunteers to draw a circle around the *r* in each of the words, such as *Caperucita, carnicero, llevarle, Feroz.*

¡OJO! In Mexico and Central America, corn on the cob *(mazorca de maíz)* is also known as *elote*.

Los lobos

BEFORE READING

Begin a chart of wolf facts with the following headings: What We Know *(Lo que sabemos)*, What We Want to Know *(Lo que queremos saber)*, and What We Learned *(Lo que aprendimos)*. Ask children to tell what they know about wolves and what they want to know. *(Díganme qué saben acerca de los lobos y qué quieren saber acerca de los lobos.)* Write their responses on the chart. Introduce the book, using the Big Book if available. Ask children to predict the type of information they will find inside.

READING

Ask children what they think they will learn by reading the book and looking at the photographs. *(¿Qué creen que aprenderán al leer el libro y mirar las fotografías?)* Point out that the text is on the left and the photographs are on the right side of each spread.

Use questions such as these to guide the reading:
- ¿En qué son similares un lobo y un perro? ¿En qué son diferentes?
- ¿Qué les gusta hacer a los lobos cuando están juntos?
- ¿Por qué y en qué forma difieren los lobos en su color?

AFTER READING

Discuss with children this factual book about wolves. Ask children to tell what they learned about wolves from the book. *(¿Qué aprendieron sobre los lobos en este libro?)* Add their responses to the chart begun in the Before Reading activity.

Response Activities

Wolf Packs
Materials: colored art paper, scissors, glue

Ask children to create a wolf mask. *(Quiero que hagan máscaras de lobos.)* Have each child cut a round head and pointed ears from a white, tan, brown, or black piece of art paper. Have them cut out eye holes and continue adding details to their masks. Then divide children into wolf packs and tell each pack to do something together that they read about in the book. *(Hagan juntos alguna actividad que leyeron en el libro.)*

Wolf Riddles
Materials: books about wolves

Have children work in pairs to create riddles *(adivinanzas)* about wolves. They may use facts from *Los lobos* or other books provided. One might write, *Vivo en un lugar cálido. Soy el lobo más pequeño. ¿Quién soy?* On the back of the page, they would write *Soy un lobo rojo*.

MINI LESSONS

• READING STRATEGY
Categorizing Information

Write the following words on the board as the heads to three columns: *El aspecto de los lobos, Lo que hacen los lobos,* and *Donde viven los lobos.* Have children review the book for facts about wolves. As they name a fact, ask them in which column you should write it.

• LANGUAGE PATTERN
Identifying Plural Words

Write the words *lobo* and *lobos* on the board or on chart paper. Ask children to tell how they know when the author is telling about more than one *(lobo, lobos)*. Compare the spelling of these two words with children. Ask them to locate other words in the book that mean more than one of something: *patas, manadas, cosas, clases, cachorros, guaridas, perros, mascotas.* Write these words on the board and ask volunteers to write the singular form beside each word.

PHONICS FOCUS

Reviewing the /b/ Sound

Review with children that the /b/ sound is represented by the letters *v* and *b*. *(El sonido de la /b/ está representado por las letras* v *y* b.) Reread the story, asking children to call out "be" every time they hear the /b/ sound. *(Cada vez que oigan el sonido /b/, digan "be".)* When you are finished reading, create two columns on the board with the headings: *v* and *b*. Say the *b* and *v* words aloud, calling on children to tell you in which column to write them. Some possible words include: *salvaje, lobos, invierno, viven, buscan, loba, vez, veces, cueva, bajo, blancos, nieve, blanca.*

Tying the Pair Together

Display copies of *Caperucita Roja y Lobo Feroz* and *Los lobos*. Ask children to tell what they learned about wolves. *(¿Qué han aprendido sobre los lobos?)* Have them describe how the books are similar and how they are different, making sure to include that *Caperucita Roja y Lobo Feroz* is a make-believe story and *Los lobos* is a book of real facts.

Movement: Caperucita Roja, Lobo Feroz
Materials: none

Have children sit in a circle. Child 1 walks around the outside of the circle and touches the others on the head, saying either *Caperucita Roja* or *Lobo*. When Child 1 says *Lobo*, Child 2 stands and chases Child 1 around the circle as he/she tries to get back to the "wolf's" seat first.

Writing: What's for Dinner?
Materials: writing paper, pencils

Working in pairs, have children list the food needed for a wolf's dinner. Have some pairs list dinner for a make-believe wolf. *(Hagan una lista de comidas para lobos de fantasía.)* Have other pairs work on listing what real wolves eat. *(Hagan una lista de comidas para lobos verdaderos.)* Then have groups compare their lists. *(Ahora comparen sus listas.)*

Creative Dramatics: Setting
Materials: posterboards, green and brown tempera paint, paint brushes

Have children look through the photos in *Los lobos* to find a setting similar to that in *Caperucita Roja y Lobo Feroz (el bosque)*. Ask pairs of children to paint a forest scene that could be used to create the setting for a play about either book. *(Hagan una pintura sobre un bosque que podría ser el ambiente para cualquiera de los dos libros.)*

ASSESSMENT

- Ask children to tell what they have learned about wolves. *(Díganme qué han aprendido sobre los lobos.)* Record and date these responses.
- Review the objectives given in the lessons for *Caperucita Roja y Lobo Feroz* and *Los lobos*. Place samples of children's work on these objectives in their portfolios.
- Use informal conferencing with children to assess reading, language, and phonics skills they have learned from the books.

For further assessment ideas and checklists, see pages 78–80.

Home Activities

Copy and distribute to children the *Llévame a casa* activity master found on page 72. Invite children to interview their families about the version of "Caperucita Roja" they remember from their childhood.

Tie It to English

LISTENING/SPEAKING/VIEWING

Reviewing Language Patterns and Sight Vocabulary
Vocabulary Words: *visit, grandmother, baker, bread, wolf, followed, help*

Go through the book *Caperucita Roja y Lobo Feroz* and introduce the vocabulary words, writing them on the board and calling on children to repeat them. Then write the following sentences on separate strips of paper, making as many copies as necessary for all the children: (1) *Caperucita Roja is going to visit her grandmother.* (2) *The baker gives her bread.* (3) *The wolf follows her.* (4) *Caperucita Roja asks the wolf for help.* (5) *The grandmother, the wolf, and Caperucita Roja eat together.* (6) *Now they are all friends.*

Divide the class into groups of three. Give each child two sentence strips. Explain that you will retell a short version of the story of Caperucita Roja in English and that they should listen carefully for the new vocabulary words. Then have each group work together to place the sentence strips in the correct order and then read them aloud to the class.

VIEWING/WRITING/SPEAKING

Distribute copies of the activity below. On a separate sheet of paper, have children make a drawing of their favorite part of the story. Encourage them to use the characters below by cutting them out and pasting them on their drawing. When children are finished, have each child talk about his or her drawing in English to the class.

LLÉVAME A CASA

Estimada familia de _____,

ACTIVIDADES SOBRE LOS LOBOS

Su niño ha estado leyendo y aprendiendo sobre los lobos y cómo viven. *Caperucita Roja y Lobo Feroz* cuenta como Caperucita usa su ingenio para cambiar al Lobo Feroz. *Los lobos* es un libro informativo sobre los diferentes tipos de lobos. Nos habla de dónde y cómo viven. Ayude a su niño a aprender más sobre los lobos escogiendo algunas de las actividades a continuación.

LIBROS ACERCA DE LOS LOBOS:

Ayude a su niño a aprender más sobre los lobos visitando la biblioteca juntos. Busquen libros como *La verdadera historia de los tres cerditos* por Jon Scieszka y *Diez cuentos de lobos* por Jean Francois Blade.

EL CINE, LA MÚSICA Y MÁS:

Vean películas sobre los lobos como, *Cry Wolf!* o *Jungle Book*. Converse con su niño sobre dónde viven los lobos y cómo sobreviven éstos. Busque canciones o rimas sobre los lobos para cantar o recitar. Un buen ejemplo es la conocida canción en inglés, "Who's Afraid of the Big Bad Wolf?"

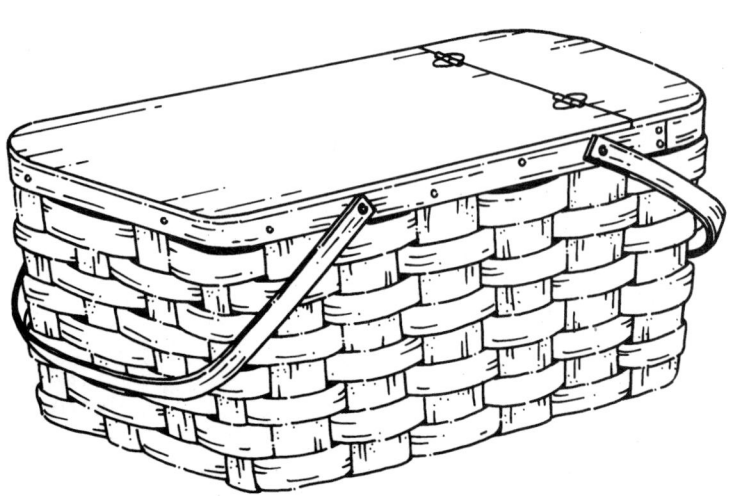

PROYECTO DE ARTE: Una cesta para el bosque

Materiales: tijeras, papel de arte, tiras recortadas de papel de arte, pegamento

Ayude a su niño a hacer una cesta para que Caperucita Roja la lleve a la casa de su abuelita. Doble una hoja de papel de arte por la mitad y haga cortes desde el doblez del centro hasta una pulgada del borde del papel. Entreteja las tiras de papel por encima y por debajo de los cortes en la hoja de papel. Pegue las tiras sueltas al papel y doble las puntas hacia arriba para formar los lados de la cesta. Póngale una manilla y haga que su niño juegue a que da un paseo por el bosque.

PARA COMPARTIR:

Pídale a su niño que cuente el cuento de Caperucita Roja y Lobo Feroz desde el punto de vista del lobo. Después que su niño haya contado el cuento, participen en un diálogo. Usted puede hacer el papel de la Caperucita o de la abuela.

Tu nombre _____

Nombra un par de libros que leíste.

⟨1⟩ _____

⟨2⟩ _____

Escribe palabras que demuestran cómo los libros son parecidos y cómo son diferentes.

Solamente en el primer libro	Lo mismo en ambos libros	Solamente en el segundo libro

Comparing Books

Tu nombre _____

Nombra un libro que leíste.

_____
_____
_____

En cada caja, dibuja a una persona o a un animal del libro. Luego escribe lo que cada uno podría decir.

Tu nombre _____

Nombra un libro que leíste.
_____
_____

Haz un dibujo para mostrar donde ocurrió.

Habla de una cosa que ocurrió en el libro.
_____
_____
_____
_____
_____

Understanding Setting and Main Idea

Tu nombre _____

Piensa en un par de libros que leíste.
Dibuja algo de verdad. Escribe **de verdad**.
Dibuja algo de fantasía.
Escribe **fantasía**.

INFORME SOBRE UN LIBRO

Tu nombre _____

Nombra un libro que leíste.
_____

_____

Colorea una de las caras en cada fila para mostrar lo que piensas.

1. ¿Cómo te gustó este libro?

2. ¿Cómo te gustó el arte o la fotografía?

3. ¿Te gustaría leer este libro de nuevo?

Responding to Books

STECK-VAUGHN *EN PAREJAS*™
Checklist for Informal Assessment

Child's name _____

Book/Print Awareness	Comments	Date
Holds book upright		
Tracks print from top to bottom of a page		
Tracks print from left to right		
Tracks print with finger, moving from word to word		
Knows when to turn a page		
Recognizes cover of book, title, and title page		
Identifies author and/or illustrator		
Recognizes high-frequency words		
Recognizes most common sight words		
Recognizes sentences		
Identifies punctuation marks		
Chooses to read independently		
Enjoys sharing stories with others		
Participates actively in shared reading activities		

Letter/Sound Knowledge	Comments	Date
Distinguishes upper and lower-case letters		
Recognizes initial sound-symbol relationships		
Recognizes final sound-symbol relationships		
Uses initial and final sounds to guess unfamiliar words		
Uses vowel sounds to decode words		
Uses blends to decode words		
Uses digraphs to decode words		
Uses letter sounds to decode words		

© Steck-Vaughn Company

STECK-VAUGHN *EN PAREJAS*™
Checklist for Informal Assessment

Child's name _____

Reading Strategies	Comments	Date
Uses pictures to retell stories in own words		
Uses illustrations or photos to help define words		
Recalls information from text		
Integrates personal experiences into reading		
Sequences events correctly		
Tells point of view		
Distinguishes between real and make-believe		
Recognizes different book formats		
Rereads for sense		
Summarizes main points or events		
Retells a story from memory		
Enjoys sharing stories with others		
Predicts events in stories		

Writing Behaviors	Comments	Date
Matches words to illustrations or drawings		
Utilizes inventive spelling		
Uses capital and lower-case letters correctly		
Uses punctuation correctly		
Replicates a text pattern		
Sequences ideas		
Uses simple sentence structures		
Integrates personal experiences into writing		
Contributes to shared writing activities		
Attempts writing of complex sentence structures		

STECK-VAUGHN *EN PAREJAS*™
Informal Conference Form

Child's Name _____   Date _____

EN PAREJAS books selected for this conference: _____

_____

Before reading the books with the child, discuss the following chart and record his or her responses.

Topic: _____

What I Know *(Lo que sé)*	What I Want to Know *(Lo que quiero saber)*

After reading the books and helping the child gather information, fill out the following chart together.

What I Learned *(Lo que aprendí)*

Ask the child the following questions:

- *¿Quién te puede ayudar a averiguar más?* _____

- *¿Dónde puedes ir para averiguar más?* _____

© Steck-Vaughn Company